IMMOVABLE ROCK

CAROLYN A. RANDALL

Foreword by
DAVID L. RANDALL

Ebookannie

ISBN: 979-8611988145
Printed in the United States of America

Scriptures are taken from:
New King James Version (NKJV): New King James Version®. Copyright © 1982 by
Thomas Nelson. Used by permission. All rights reserved.

Holy Bible, New International Version®, NIV® Copyright ©1973, 1978, 1984, 2011 by
Biblica, Inc. ® Used by permission. All rights reserved worldwide.

English Standard Version (ESV): The Holy Bible, English Standard Version
Copyright © 2001 by Crossway Bibles, a publishing ministry of Good News
Publishers.

New American Standard Bible (NASB): Copyright © 1960, 1962, 1963, 1968, 1971, 1972,
1973, 1975, 1977, 1995 by The Lockman Foundation.

New International Version (NIV): Holy Bible, New International Version®, NIV®
Copyright ©1973, 1978, 1984, 2011 by Biblica, Inc. ® Used by permission. All rights
reserved worldwide.

Graphic Design, Ebookannie, www.ebookannie.com
Photography, Carolyn A. Randall

Disclaimer: The opinions expressed in our published works are those of the author
and do not reflect the opinions of Ebookannie or its editors. The publisher does not
assume any liability for author's personal, requested, and preferred editing styles,
punctuation, grammar, and syntax.

To my wonderful husband Dave who found me the perfect beach on Cape Cod where I could talk with God. To my son's Anthony and Dan and my beautiful daughter-in-law's Jeanine and Courtney who gave me love and encouragement to write this story. To my wonderful grandchildren Aria, William, Cierra, John, Caleb and Caden to continue to follow in the footsteps of their parents. To my brother and sister and all the DiFalco clan that they may read and understand the life I choose.

"And the Lord said, "Here is a place by Me, and you shall stand on the rock. So it shall be, while My glory passes by, that I will put you in the cleft of the rock, and will cover you with My hand while I pass by.

— Exodus 33:21-22

FOREWORD

As we go through this life there are many people that we meet. Very few have an impact in ways that touch our lives forever from knowing them. Carolyn Ann Randall was such a person. When she walked into a room, the fragrance of Jesus exuded from her. Her infectious smile was filled with joy and love. His *shalom* was all over her and could not be denied. She had been with God.

Carolyn was a prayer warrior. Many people would feel her prayers as she would lay prone on the floor for hours. There are so many stories I could share about her prayers as she prayed to the Holy Spirit for God's intervention into many lives.

In the Fall of 2002, I found her a special place at a private beach on Cape Cod. Shortly thereafter, I lost her to a beach. She walked the beach alone with Jesus for hours talking to the King. This was no longer a religion, but a relationship with God.

She looked forward each year going to Cape Cod. At first, it was a week. Then, the following year, it was two weeks. Then, it became a month. Her final time at Cape Cod was spent writing her book all summer. At the end of the beach, there was an outcropping of glacial boulders. One of these boulders had split in half. She called this boulder her "Cleft in the Rock," and there she would write for hours. Her pen name was the "Sandpiper."

I love you Sandpiper and I'll see you again one day.

Your loving husband,

Dave

1
————

ON THE ROAD AGAIN

BURNING HEARTS

"And they said one to another, 'Did not our heart burn within us,
while he talked with us by the way, and while he opened to us the
scriptures?'"
—LUKE 24:32

To Georgia? To Damascus? To Emmaus? To Samaria? The old saying, *'all roads lead to Rome'* emerges. However, all roads should lead to Calvary—its riveting truths, its powerful promises, its eternal hope of glory.

When traveling to Georgia, there are billboards that display "Jesus is the Answer," "He is eternal life," and "Call listed phone number for TRUTH." Are these signs read or even noticed as traffic rushes by on its way to somewhere? The query persists if 'somewhere' packages the TRUTH so needed by the world. This TRUTH of Jesus is incomparable, inexhaustible, unparalleled and inextinguishable. It is totally complete. It is entirely all the length, breadth and depth of the "I AM".

How many billboards have you rushed by on your way to somewhere with a 'someday I'll' attitude? 'Someday I'll' consider this Jesus person. 'Someday I'll' read the Bible to see His life come alive through prophecies of old and gospels of the apostles. 'Someday I'll' slow down adequately enough—maybe even get in the breakdown lane—to give serious thought to this Savior who re-invented history, turned the world upside-down, left people gasping in His time and leaving people today groping to validate centuries of recorded events.

When traveling to Georgia, there are roadways filled with vehicles of intricate design and complex mechanics to display tremendous creativity and intelligence. These talents are good things. Just imagine the strength of these same resources being transformed by the power of Jesus. It could just put billboards out of business. What a heavenly thought!

What notices were advertised while Silas, Paul, was galloping to Damascus? Certainly not messages of redemption and resurrection. His horse did not pull over to an exit offering Living Water (Revelation 21:6) and daily Bread (Matthew 6:11).

Like so many who resist and question Christ's validity and identity, it is not until they fall off their high horses and are brought to their knees that they can they realize the deception of their environment. Unlike the Emmaus travelers, opportunity might not be available for a second chance. The horse riders remain adamant and prevail, as Silas, to negate and overturn the obvious facts and truths of Jesus incarnate, resurrected and sitting at the right hand of the Father. They are invincible and indomitable, so they think. One can only pray they are overcome in their spirit and manifest.

 And he trembling and astonished said Lord, what will you have me do?"

— ACTS 9:6

For reference sake, and a short synopsis, Paul is blinded for three days until God employs Ananias, which means *Jehovah has been gracious*, to lay hands on Paul to restore his sight. The rest of the story truly is history. Paul, for the remainder of his life, proclaimed and taught that Christ is the Son of God. Oh! To have this occasion repeat itself now, in this present day. The difference between Paul and future 'horse riders' is a matter of centuries.

Time was on Paul's side. Such luxury is not available today. Jesus is coming back soon—not in centuries, not in eons—but soon.

Pray the Damascus experience will encounter the resistant, the proud, and the invincible.

There were no single engine planes pulling banners with large letters displaying the "Good News" of the resurrection miracle to assuage the questioning and 'unbelief' of the two disciples walking to Emmaus (Luke 24:25, 26).

 Did not our heart burn within us, while he talked with us by the way, and while he opened to us the scriptures?

— LUKE 24:32

"Are you a stranger in Jerusalem? Do you not know what happened to Jesus the prophet?" Although they traveled and ministered with Jesus for three years and He had told them God's plan for salvation, which necessitated His death, burial and resurrection (Luke 18:31-34), they could not get their minds wrapped around the reality of it all (Psalm 119:25).

It was only later at dinner they recognized Jesus and asked, "...did our hearts not burn within us when He spoke."

Only then did they recall all the wonders and miracles they experienced. Oh! To have the vulnerable, needy hearts of this present culture 'burn' with the impact of Jesus. For many, it will be too late to invite Him to dinner and receive illumination about Him. Many will continue walking in the dust of Emmaus not realizing Christ is right beside them.

> This is an emotional Jesus wanting desperately to be recognized; wanting desperately to be understood for the love He displayed on the cross—for them, for all; wanting desperately not to wait until dinner to be acknowledged.
>
> — CAROLYN RANDALL

One description of God is God of the second chance. For many, Emmaus is the only second chance offered to bring the doubters home or those who want to believe but are waiting for the 'burn' in their hearts.

Going to the well was only one direction out of town not requiring the thirsty, scorned woman to heed road signs to find her way to the man from Galilee who just happened to reprogram His GPS to wait for her.

Even the disciples questioned the satellite reading the Lord was using. Is there not a better way to get to Jerusalem and bypass Samaria? In modern language is there not a better route? But Jesus knew the woman's past and the long route her life had traveled. He was aware of her route that day, in the heat of high noon, would be the shortest path she ever walked. After meeting Jesus, she was set free, her thirst satisfied with the Living Water which would keep her healed, well and whole.

Do you know someone who needs encouragement to be 'on that road' to the well to be set free from a past of shame, loneliness and feeling hopeless?

If so, reach out in prayer. Whatever actions God prescribes, He desires that none should perish. Think of your life before the Savior climbed into the tabernacle of your heart and transformed you forever.

The present culture sits in a lap of information. In a world infused with all varieties of GPS and media, there is no regard for signs, exits and billboards. Amazing the contrast and contradiction of communication streaming down for centuries since Christ was born, died, and rose again. Do we need to fall off our high horses? Collect pebbles and sand in our sandals? Or be so desperately parched and thirsty we are finally brought to our knees?

There must be an urgency to get back on the road again—Calvary Road whose end displayed all the hopes and promises of a sovereign and mighty God. The road was dirty and dusty, splattered in red with Jesus' blood. The cross was devastating in its' brutality. Yet, for all the anguish and fear represented, a hope was birthed—a promise was fulfilled.

"Today my Son will be with me in heaven."

God is holding this same promise for us as we approach being 'on the road again' in our lives—traveling our journeys' roads, secure in God's promises of eternal life. Be secure. Trust God's faithfulness. Get off the horse, strap on the sandals and walk to the well of Living Water and be free.

2

GOD, CAN I BORROW THE CAR?

ASK HIM

*"He saith unto them, But whom say ye that I am? And Simon Peter
answered and said, Thou art the Christ, the Son of the living God."*
—Matthew 16:15-16

Learning can be difficult at any age. Particularly, being older.
Not because the brain is phasing out or the body is fading
away and mental acuity has changed. It is more likely due to not
inquiring of the Father, first and foremost, for all decisions necessary
in life's later journeys.

In accumulating experiences of challenges and trials and victories,
there is a tendency to not follow Jesus' example that everything He
did was first inquired of the Father. What better illustration to follow?
What better teacher than Jesus?

Who do you say I am? Who is Christ for us today? Read Letters from
Cell 92: Part 2, "Who is Christ for us today?"[1]

Haunting questions require soul-searching answers. Answers from
the Father. However, He must be sought, not only to ensure permis-

sion of His will, but to show admiration and adoration to Him from Whom all blessings flow.

If Christ sought the Father fervently and repeatedly, what other sensible choice remains? It is a choice, which results in calm and peace by eliminating doubt. However, assumption prevails. Provision in place. Keys on the counter. Car in garage.

Surely it is okay to take off and carry out our agendas. Why else would God have keys and car available if not to use them? He has allowed their use in the past, so it should be okay to borrow the car again now.

How quick to forget Jesus' approach of always asking the Father for His next actions. The Psalms implore to *'incline our ear to him'*, and *'lean on His understanding.'* And yet, recklessly, we act improperly to the above questions.

In conversation, we respond similar to Peter and profoundly claim Jesus is the Resurrected Savior, Our Lord.

There is the firm belief that Christ is for us, in all ways, supported by very good biblical lip service.

But the car is not just a nice commodity. It is an illustration wooing us to come to our Father and ask: "Is it okay?"

Is it your will and desire to take a certain action, to pursue a particular situation, instead of picking up the keys and putting the car in drive?

It is well known that the Father is the Giver of all gifts (James 1:17). He is a generous Father with His provisions desiring to bless abundantly (Psalm 65:11)—whether it is the bowls of heaven spilling their contents over our lives or the lamb in the thicket in times of great need. The stories are endless, not only those contained in His Word, but also events which happen in our lives. We are living testimonies of His goodness extended through all of life's journeys.

If Christ is known as the Resurrected Savior, then mortal thinking should be skewed to accept His omnipotence; believe in the power of God raising Him from the dead and reigning in the heaven-lies.

His death and ascension, challenged and investigated for centuries, has been proven by the best of unbelieving skeptics. So the question persists.

> Who is Christ for us today? Who is this Christ incarnated for an earthly mission to redeem mankind back to Him and the Father.

What kind of love leaves the portals of heaven to be a Babe in a stinky trough of hay; to walk the dusty roads to meet with sinners and derelicts of society; to forsake all at Calvary so we would not be forsaken because of sin?

This God-man who taught and travelled with the culture of His time, and yet, He never forgot the Father.

Known for His miracles and parables, but should be profoundly known for teaching, that in all circumstances, first and foremost, He went to the Father.

In His own right He possessed jurisdiction to act independently of any other superior, but inquiring of the Father was a lesson, a way of life critical for mankind. A critical application for running the race and finishing well. He and the Father want us to run with fervor and finish jubilantly, not limping or dragging across the line.

Who do we say He is? How much do we trust Him to be Christ for us all days, in all ways?

How badly do we want to borrow the car? Enough to enact the right approach and ask Abba, Father?

Haggai lamented:

> Now therefore thus saith the Lord of hosts; Consider your ways. Ye have sown much, and bring in little; ye eat, but ye have not enough; ye drink, but ye are not filled with drink; ye clothe you, but there is none warm; and he that earneth wages earneth wages to put it into a bag with holes. Thus saith the Lord of hosts; Consider your ways.
>
> — HAGGAI 1:5-7

Consider your ways. Be mindful that the One who created creation also created in us an urgency to be obedient to follow His directives. Let us not deny or avoid the privilege and right protocol so there will be peace in our lives and eternal satisfaction and satiation.

Sounds like a big God to me.

A God constantly juggling the balance of the universe and, yet, is ready available, and desiring. We approach him with the query —*"God, can I borrow the car?"*

3

PILLOW ON THE FLOOR

PART 1

"And when He had sent the multitudes away, He went up on the mountain by Himself to pray. Now when evening came, He was alone there."
—MATTHEW 14:23

It has been said, when praying, it is the posture of the heart more so than a certain position of the body, a situation illuminated to me when my health took a detour.

For years when health was not an issue, anytime, any place, any form of stature could work—standing, sitting, kneeling for a long time, but, of late, certain alignments did not cooperate with my skeletal frame. Not being able to 'pitch forward' like sitting at a picnic table, a straight up perpendicular position is necessary. Necessity, the mother of invention, has led to the 'pillow on the floor'.

Enter in large, cushy pillow on the floor near a big chair or even the sideboard of my bed to sit upright. Voilà!

No excuses remain to get God's attention. Of course, in reality, it is He always yearning for our attention:

The position of our heart.

I doubt He cares about sitting, standing, walking; chairs, cushions, church pews. After all, Jesus, His Son, His "right-hand man" had only a rock to lean against in Gethsemane. And there were probably similar options when Jesus left the disciples and the crowds to go to the mountain (Matthew 14:23) to pray.

Actually, praying, leaning against a rock, is a privileged location offered by our Father. True, it is not Gethsemane but, with the thanks to my benevolent Father (and although far, far away), I have an actual rock to pray on at a certain beach.

It is with that actual, physical experience and memory I can accept sitting on a cushion on the floor, which reemphasizes praying, is a position of the heart, not comfort or a certain orchestrated place.

Carolyn's favorite rock at Cold Storage Beach

God makes praying 'easy' because He is available and approachable 24/7. It is we who rationalize time, reinvent the wheel, and redirect our priorities that make prayer challenging. Not God.

When we are willing to focus on Him and not our selfish agendas, He provides everything we need—a rock, a pillow, the floor, a garden. He customizes our environment like a good tailor fits clothing. Like good tailoring, we need to look sharp, to look fit, not to fool ourselves but the enemy whose hand is on the throttle of distraction; just waiting for us 'to get in place' and then set up His lures of weariness, rabbit-trail thoughts, coincidental calls or interruptions.

How often I have thought I would have been a good disciple because of falling sleep—sleep which usually avoids me when going to bed—but becomes a willing accomplice at times of prayer.

> How often I have thought I have been 'part of the crowd' wanting Jesus to do His miracles instead of realizing this example of getting away to pray was the miracle I really needed?

Why did I often walk to the wells in my life at high noon with an empty bucket instead of acknowledging His presence where I already was, regardless of my tainted soul?

Oh! To live out, enact, enforce the old song: "Sweet Hour of Prayer" [1] that calls me from a world of care and bids me at my Father's throne. Not that God sets a timer for it is known of Him that a day is like a thousand years or years are like a day. Hour of Prayer! And then to add sweetness to it! Talk about amazing grace to accomplish such a challenge. God appreciates any and all devoted and dedicated time without setting boundaries of minutes and hours. It is we who must learn not 'to fit Him into' our calendars, devices and blackberries.

> God appreciates any and all devoted and dedicated time without setting boundaries of minutes and hours.

Prayer should be, in some ways, like a baseball game with no predetermined time lengths. Although the game has some structure, there are no time outs, quarter or half times, no intermission. It is played until a team wins, even if requiring extra innings. How often have the demands or monotonous routines of life caused us to 'strike out' and not score well when prayer is regarded, let alone going extra innings? Where is the error? Where is the force out?

Prayer is the game of life.

From Jesus' example it should be obvious that prayer, quality prayer, is the game of life.

Quality does not equate to quantity. Sincerity is not measured by a clock or game rules or yardsticks.

God desires our relationship with Him to have value, to be set apart from our daily absorption of living life and offering Him quality time centered on Him and Him alone—not shared with or lessened by other wants.

His pattern of prayer, Psalm 27:4,[2] indulges us to be sincere and available always, to maintain a quality of conversing or listening with Him daily, routinely, habitually and thereby eliminating giving Him the leftovers of our time or waiting until an emergency or crisis.

So many tragedies of history portray a people 'turning to God' when the unexpected, especially horrific, happens. Suddenly, God is asked to appear and perform a miracle, or questioned, like Mary and Martha, why there was no earlier intervention to prevent a calamity.

Gosh! When I reflect back on certain occurrences, could things have been different if my heart had been positioned better in prayer?

Could I have had more grace or mercy to people involved?

Could there have been a different, maybe better, outcome if I was in position in His tabernacle? I do not know.

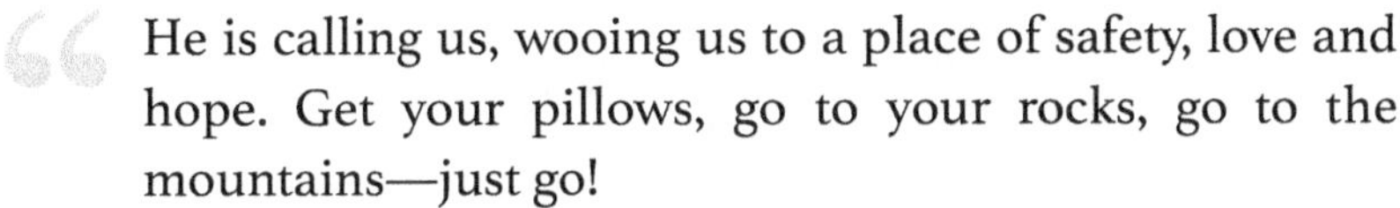

> The important thing for me to learn is to be aware of the necessity and validity of prayer—particularly when the drought is long, the knees are calloused, the anticipated hope slowly leaking out like a shrinking balloon.

As I previously mentioned, prayer needs to be like a baseball game with no boundaries of time. We pray to the end.

We do not end in a tie with the devil.

We win. He loses.

We pray. God wins. God is the Victor. We pray.

We are humbled—and also victorious; victorious knowing the quality of our hearts and our intentions has put a smile on God's face. He is pleased we have been exposed to a Gethsemane experience and not caught sleeping. He, from whom all blessings flow, has given us life, His Son, the Holy Spirit, the actual air we breathe.

Can we not return to Him 'sweet hour of prayer' whether that hour equates to a few minutes or hours, a day or a night?

Can we not establish our hearts to reprogram our minds' thoughts to let Him take us captive—into His tabernacle, into His sanctuary— where true peace and rest exist?

> He is calling us, wooing us to a place of safety, love and hope. Get your pillows, go to your rocks, go to the mountains—just go!

Let us emulate Jesus as much as this mortal flesh will allow. If prayer secured Him to the Father, because of Calvary, we will be made secure also. God's security is eternal, not temporary or able to be destroyed by the world.

He is making us an offer we should not refuse.

The world is full of four letter words so contradictory to God's kingdom. But God has a four-letter word vocabulary that, being a good tailor, fits all of us.

Pray. Hope. Pray. Have.

4

PILLOW ON THE FLOOR

PART 2

*"But you, when you pray, enter into your closet, and when you
have shut the door, pray to the Father which is in secret."*
—MATTHEW 6:6

I love it! A beautiful, young friend claims her stationary bike is her prayer closet. A beautiful, older friend, whose daily domain is the confinement of a wheel chair, is always in her prayer closet. My 'closet' seasons have been kneeling at the corner of a dining room table, walking a beach in Cape Cod, framing the black nights in a wilderness. Would make for an interesting inventory to survey all the varied locations and descriptions of prayer closets, some more appealing, or spiritual than others, but all effective. A mountaintop, a gurgling brook, an antique rocking chair, etc., cast a more luring appeal than a prison cell, a wheelchair, and the refuge of a bathroom to escape the clamor of family life. However, as in all areas of life, God is not bound by geography, structures, or gilded thrones.

Matthew 6:6, *"But you, when you pray, enter into your closet, and when you have shut the door, pray to the Father which is in secret."*

To repeat a previously used phrase: 'it is the position of the heart' which transitions any application of prayer.

A stationary bike could be symbolic of hearts and minds pedaling to get away from daily detours to enter God's tabernacle. Sitting, staying in one place, to represent the 'sitting' of our hearts to remain intact and focused on him.

Obviously, a bike is not applicable to everyone. That is why God, in His sovereignty, does not limit our choices; if anything, He expands them to fit our needs, personalities and ways of life. The 'praying' miles of a walker or runner are jubilant because it is such a one-on-one with God. Each step, each mile is a prayer sent up to the throne of God. Personally, in the miles I walked, it was a great release of not just saying: "Oh, God, here is my list of what I would like you to do", instead the barriers of demands were usually replaced by a quieting of my rabbit-trail thinking so I could hear Him. I could receive His thoughts coming down and not the usual one-way direction of my stuff going up to Him.

It is a two way street with God, but only one lane, each of us taking a turn. However, we need to allow him space and quiet to receive His directives and travel the lane coming down from him to us.

In addition to setting a physical tone, 'shutting the door' implies turning off the hydrant of thoughts coursing through our minds like shooting stars , one thought bombarding into another. Obviously, God would anticipate this situation when the Psalmist scribed:

"Be still, and know I am God."

— PSALM 46:10

Notice the sequence. Be still, first, then you can know God. Be still. Physically and emotionally. Whoa! What a concept inn this hurried, fast-paced, multi-tasked society.

Be still? Me? The ever-ready drum-beating bunny?

What a task to learn the process of 'stillness' defined in God's terms.

What an undertaking it is to prepare first physically, then emotionally, a location and mindset in which God could enter and have my full attention. Surely there must be room for a few of my important stray thoughts or dangling dainties.

It was a determined learning process to see my involvement gauge go to empty so He could fill; to stop running ambitiously from one activity to another regardless of their importance; to re-categorize priorities so God would be first.

Seek ye first the kingdom of God. By seeking Him first, all other obligations and tasks fell into place, into alignment, so there would be no helter-skelter.

Turn off me. Turn on God

That was the key. Even though odd.

It was somewhere in this early phase of my journey that Psalm 42, Psalm 63 and Psalm 27:4 became life and breath to me. The words, the intent of God's Psalmist, to portray the needs of my heart and the anticipated provisions of protection, healing and safety to produce a profound result of 'how' I needed to know God.

The quiet and solitude of a prayer closet was mandatory if I was to 'know Him'; to genuinely know His attributes and consider their effects on my walk; to understand 'abiding in the Vine'.

I must give credit to where credit is due. Mentors.

There were two beautiful ladies whose patience wore long, determined and very thick to take this fledgling under their wings and provide counsel and direction. "Pillars". And Pillars they were.

Truly, these Daughters of the King had walked the walk, lived the walk through their own victories, triumphs, trials and defeats. They explained the vocabulary of God: choice words like prayer, sanctuary, abiding, steadfastness.

Above all, was God's faithfulness through any and all of my pursuits. Heaven was definitely gifted when these Pillars went on to glory. Hopefully, I will see them again—once I get over being stunned by seeing Jesus. And it will probably be them who will pick me up and get me steady on my feet.

There is an old be-bop song, To Know Him Is to Love Him,[1] by The Teddy Bears.

To Know Him Is to Love Him
The Teddy Bears
Lyrics by Amy Winehouse

To know know know him
Is to love love love him
Just to see that smile
Makes my life worthwhile

To know know know him
Is to love love love him
And I do, and I do, and I do

Oh I'll be good to him
I'll bring joy to him oh oh
Everyone says there'll come a day
When I'll walk alongside of him

To know know know him
Is to love love love him
And I do, I really do, and I do

Why can't he see?
How blind here he be?
Someday he'll see
That he was meant just for me, oh oh oh oh

To know know know him
Is to love love love him
Just to see that smile
Makes my life worthwhile

To know know know him
Is to love love love him
And I do, I really do, and I do

Talk about amazing grace! Going from be-bop music to baptism in the Spirit. But that is what the 'closet' does. It pushes aside stuff on our shelves clogging our way; stuff hanging up to surround us. A clear path is made, as others have stated, for a vertical liaison: we reaching up to God, but more importantly, we allowing and accepting Him reaching down to us.

Yes, life is all about choices.

We all fall short of always making right choices at the right time —victims of our flesh and frailties. However, God is a God of the second chance and fortunately, for most of us, several chances.

> He will never stop loving us so much to prevent our hearts and minds to choose Him, learn of His ways and make Him Lord of our lives.

Like the prodigal son's father, He is always scanning the horizon— cloak and ring ready—to welcome us home; to bring us into His sanctuary; to be secured in His pavilion; to have ready a grand feast.

Therefore, is it not a concerted effort to prepare quality 'closet' time well worth our endeavors?

Well worth going to Him regardless of how ragged and world worn we are to find solace and possible answers or solutions to questions that overwhelm or astound our lives?

We need to prepare—not full of theological dialogue but, as the hart, to be thirsty, wanting to drink in His brook of healing; to go hungry to feast on His fulfilling attributes. To truly 'be still; and 'to know him' as our God.

Calvary and closets—two powerful Gifts from a sovereign God, a loving Abba Father, who loves His children so.

Calvary and closets equal love. The blood spattered road to the cross. The quiet and seclusion of a prayer closet.

By comparison they are extreme; however, both serve to display the desire and need to seek the Father—for trust and obedience—to accept and perform His will.

Everyone's 'cup' is different (although some brim to devastating limits) uniquely and personally designed by God. We doubt our capabilities to accept and endure, to be strong and courageous, yet all the while He is preparing our hearts for profound faith to believe the walls will fall down, the sea will part, the lions will be stilled.

He is infusing Nehemiah faith to remain on our walls, placing one brick after another, and not 'come down' until our work is done. The wall is daunting and the bricks may become heavier increasing our need ever more for 'closet' time as He completes His work in us.

> "Being confident of this very thing, that he which has begun a good work in you will perform it (continue to do so) until the day of Jesus Christ."

> — PHILIPPIANS 1:6

All this rhetoric to say—**find a closet.** Be faithful to it. Ask God to supply the decision, determination and discipline to follow through —follow through to find a place in Him that will detour doubts, create courage, reassure resurrection rewards, and enliven eternity. As the five virgins were prepared with oil filled lamps, let us be prepared to have our lamps full—especially when Jesus returns.

Poured in the Oil and The Wine [2]
"He poured in the oil and the wine
The kind that restoreth my soul
He found me bleeding and dying on the Jericho Road
And He poured in the oil and the wine"

Luke 22:15, "And He said unto them, with desire (I have wanted very much) I have desired to eat this Passover with you...." Although this particular verse relates to the last supper Jesus shared with His disciples, it is still God, our Father, who desires to sup with us; to commune with us; to be with us; to nestle us in His tabernacle; to open wide any style of closet door to have fellowship with him. This is an on going extended invitation.

Let our prayer closets be the RSVP He so desires.

Let our prayer closets reflect the honor and privilege granted to us— that the God of Creation, the King of the Universe, is not too busy, too pre-occupied to meet us wherever and whenever we choose.

Let us be appreciative of His Gift of a free will and return it back to him with honor and praise and much thanksgiving.

Let us establish in our own immediate world a place of intimacy with the Trinity—Father, Son and Holy Spirit—so, when the door is opened and we exit, we have been changed; we can be the salt 'testimony' (Matthew 5:13a, 14a— "You are the salt of the earth; You are the light of the world...)

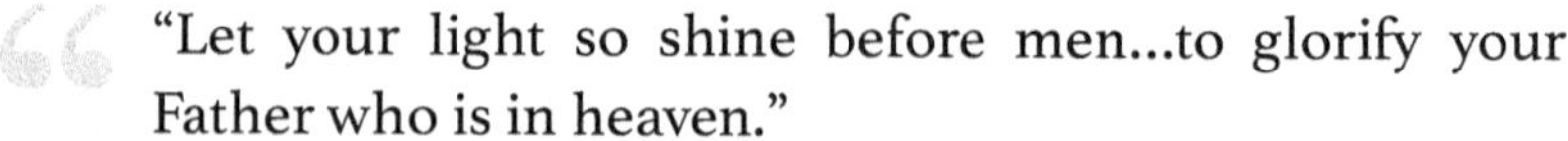 "Let your light so shine before men...to glorify your Father who is in heaven."

— MATTHEW 5:16

As in everything in all our lives, the driving concept is: It is His story, for His glory and we are just the characters in the plot. Let us play out our roles well for He is the Author and Finisher of our faith. Let us emphatically believe that concept and live out that description of him.

5

———

CUTTING THE RIBBON

LOOK UP AND LET GO

"And when these things begin to come to pass, then look up, and lift up your heads; for your redemption draweth nigh."
—LUKE 21:28

Snip. The ribbon having tethered the balloon was cut. Away. Away. In a fraction of a millisecond the balloon took flight over rooftops, trees and headed east. Release. Freedom. Independent, no longer attached to an object, which limited the heights, it could achieve. Now, as a bird leaving its nest, the balloon could soar without constriction.

Obviously, its landing place is unknown—or did it land at all? Keeping it in clear view for two minutes, it seemed to be enjoying its 'wings' lifting it higher and higher. Soon, to the natural eye, it became a black dot like the floaters in eyes with cataracts. The big, round, colorful balloon changed to a black dot actually hidden in a cloud not to be seen again.

Did the balloon take with it the negative strongholds firmly tethered to the owner? Would it keep floating until its air finally leaked out, become defenseless and landing somewhere in an earthly location?

Will it land in a tree near a house and be a watchman (like the blood over the doorposts) to safeguard the people within? Its final destination will never be known.

What of our destinations?

Snip. What balloons are in our lives?

Snip. What ribbons need to be cut?

Snip. What release and freedom is needed so we can soar?

Snip. It only takes a snip from Jesus to set people free, to rise and let them soar.

Balloons possess a world of their own. Large. Colorful. Round. Long. Square. Although balloons themselves represent happy thoughts and occasions, it is the tethering emphasized here. A string clutched so tightly in a child's hand or a ribbon tied to a stationary object to keep it in place and not fly away.

Snip. Jesus has scissors in hand waiting to cut the ribbons commanding and demanding our attitudes and actions, our responses and reactions.

Snip. What of balloons in our lives? What balloons are we tethering of poor attitudes, unforgiveness, lack of self-control, impatience, selfishness and other behaviors totally opposite the Fruits of the Spirit?

Why? Why allow such negativities that result in discord, disruption, chaos and confusion? Are we deceived by the balloons appearance of merriment to allow us to live a façade? To live in a world veneered by achievement and distraction so we can avoid confessing our need for God and the healing only He can provide?

Snip. What ribbons need to be cut?

Ribbons which take on a persona of cords, ropes and chains, anything to weight us down and confine us to the prisons inside our minds and thoughts. A very old song by Russ Taff, Praise the Lord[1], has lyrics stating,

When you're up against a struggle
that shatters all your dreams
And your hopes have been cruelly crushed
by Satan's manifested schemes
And you feel the urge within you
to submit to earthly fears
Don't let the faith you're standing
in seem to disappear

Praise the Lord,
He can work through those who praise Him
Praise the Lord,
for our God inhabits praise
Praise the Lord,
for the chains that seems to bind you
Serve only to remind you
that they drop powerless behind you
When you praise Him

Now Satan is a liar and
he wants to make us think
That we are paupers when he knows
himself we're children of the King
So lift up the mighty shield of faith
for the battle must be won
We know that Jesus Christ has risen
so the work's already done

Praise the Lord,
He can work through those who praise Him

> *Praise the Lord,*
> *for our God inhabits praise*
> *Praise the Lord,*
> *for the chains that seems to bind you*
> *Serve only to remind you*
> *that they drop powerless behind you*
> *When you praise Him"*

Like peering into the bottom of a narrow vase, we need to take a deep, inward look of our 'ribbon' inventory—whether a simple string of an annoying habit or a heavy metal chain linked by damaging behavior.

We need to acknowledge an omniscient God who, not only knows all the ribbons, but is the only One, the only God who can snip them and bring healing. Hours of meditating while walking a labyrinth only add to the delusion our souls live in and bring no cure. Occupying our time to volunteer to notable organizations; to be involved with reliable ministries extending help to others and other energy absorbing activities only veneer our emotions without reaching down deep into our needs.

Like cutting off a dandelion at ground level. The head might be gone, but the tenacious root determinedly stays buried deep into the ground.

Snip. Hand Jesus the scissors to unleash your tethering.

Snip. What release and freedom is needed so we can soar?

Not to accumulate 'more' as the present culture dictates and demands, but to soar to accomplishments God has pre-ordained, pre-designed, pre-designated for us, not as a hard task master, but as a caring and loving God—a compassionate Father—who 'girds us up' to be excellent, not perfect, as possible, even though living in this mortal flesh. Snip. How often have we lowered the ceilings in our lives, the heights of our expectations challenged by a world system that is good, at best, but exclusively only temporal? Instead of listening to His voice calling us to paths with guarantees, there is a tendency to worry more about people's reactions and our reputations than to regard His eternal promises.

Reminds me of the boys going to Emmaus—these two apostles who lived in the circle of Jesus' influence for three years—but had doubts and questions, (without search engines like Google and Safari), of the miraculous resurrection weekend.

Not surprising, Jesus questioned the tethering of their own thinking. Little were they aware that Jesus was bringing scissors to dinner that night. Snip. Eyes opened. Hearts a flamed. Of course, as we know, the rest is history how the church soared from this scraggly band of eleven men. Established locally. Grown globally. A balloon let go to all the world, not bound by geographical borders.

Snip. Let Jesus blow the roofs off our constricting negative ceilings. Let those shingles of habits and behaviors, addictions and attitudes fall off and release us to freedom by abiding in him.

Look up. Our redemption draws nigh.

Look up. See the balloons carrying away, never to return, our imperfections and impurities of life. Pledge your allegiance to the Lamb, Jesus.

He was in the thicket, at the well, on Calvary's Road, on the cross.

He was in the upper room. He was on the shore of Galilee.

He is in our lives, scissors in hand, to SNIP and make us free.

6

TEN GIFTS FROM GOD

IN THE MOMENT

*"The Lord is my Rock and my fortress and my deliverer; my God,
my strength, in whom I will trust, my buckler, and the horn of my
salvation and my high tower."*
—PSALM 18:2

Do these Gifts not exemplify *"Who is Christ for me today?"* These gifts are such a profound assurance of Christ being in every detail of my life—the challenges and the blessings.

The intense dimensions of these Gifts is the verb used: IS—not was, or maybe—but IS, which means always available, always approachable, always assuring. God has always been of the moment starting with the creation. Genesis 1:1, "In the beginning," He always was and always will be, but more importantly and emphatically, He IS now. There is no need for a special calendar event or waiting for a particular alignment of moon and stars and heavens. God IS.

He claimed in the beginning He was the "I AM" and He has remained faithful and true to that promise. However, even with such endorsement, He chooses to embellish that promise into different characteristics to carry us through our lives' journeys.

My Rock. As a rock, He is my refuge, a solid foundation to build faith on—a foundation that is stable, which does not waiver when the wind blows (Matthew 7:24,25). For me personally, He has blessed me with an actual rock—a tangible sentry on my favorite beach. Formidable. Huge. Always present. Regardless of the view, the rock takes center place in any vision of the shore. The water ebbs and flows with the undaunted presence of the rock. It remains. It is possible to touch it, feel its' smoothness and sense its' rugged determination to consistently safeguard the area. It is unmovable. As is God. Too big, center place in our lives as life's challenges ebb and flow and He remains the focus point in any view.

My Fortress. The image illuminates structures seemingly impenetrable like the wall around Jerusalem, the dominance of the Louvre museum, massive structures throughout Europe having endured centuries of attacks by man and the elements. Yet, they remain. As does God. God looms in circumstances to portray an impenetrable wall the enemy cannot damage or take. Our salvation is kept in tack. Our integrity is held together as adversities appear and rear their ugly heads, but to no avail.

My Deliverer. "...and deliver us from evil.." The familiar phrase from the Lord's Prayer tucked between two verses saying beforehand " lead us not into temptation.." and followed by "for thine is the kingdom and power and glory forever.." To deliver us from evil—to rescue us in trials when the waters are rising and there seems no way to dam them because they keep spilling into our lives. First we ask to not be led into temptation because we know our flesh is weak. God also knows. He delivers us from the temptation so we can regroup, and realign ourselves with His Word. As if deliverance would not be enough on its own, He then says, believe, take hope, "for mine is the kingdom and the power and the glory forever." He delivers not only from temptation and trial but then, as a bonus, He makes provision for us in His kingdom, which will exist forever.

My God. God, the omnipotent One, all omniscient, all omnipresent, all holy, all truth, everlasting, the Holy One of Israel, the Creator of all things—mankind, nature, the universe—and yet He says: I AM your God—personal, big, real, forever. With our finite nature, with our flaws, with our human tendencies to run the gamut and yet we can claim him as our God. He makes himself known to us through Christ. He inhabits our praises. He tells us He is our Abba, Father, and, because of Christ and through Christ we can petition him with our needs, and yes, even our wants. We "incline our ear to him" and He hears our hearts' cries. Sounds like a pretty big, colossal God.

My Strength. Power. Staunch. Endurance. Trust. "For when I am weak, He is strong" Oh! The times considering our strengths would be adequate to keep us girded up to defeat the enemy not realizing the silliness of our foolishness. God's strength is staunch, full of power, always enduring and always trustworthy. He will never slack, get weary, fade away or not be dependable. As the song sings: "God is good all the time.." especially in those trials that will beset us, that will sap our energy, weaken our determination to remain in the fight. He endures 'to the end' (John 13:1) teaching trust and dependence on Him. He is like the mighty Redwoods resistant to the elements for centuries. He stands.

I Will Trust. It is a choice to trust God. And in today's fractured society, trust is rarely to be found and kept in tack and reliable. There has to be confidence in something that is genuine, to provide safety, a shelter when the winds blow and the storms rage. Since the pair, Adam and Eve were deceived in the Garden by an apple, mankind has always been on the brink to trust humanness. The best of intentions, the depths of relationships with families and friends cannot guarantee one hundred per cent to never falter (for we are all sinners). So what is the anchor that needs to be dropped? God's trust. God says: "come all ye who are heavy laden and I will give you rest." The 'rest' is the result of "in whom I will trust". Rest, like peace, does not come easily for all of us who have inherited the outcome of the

Garden experience. Trust certainly does not come, not capable of, from the world with its' fragmented mentality and much self-centered thinking. Genuine, one hundred per cent trust can only come from God who is the same yesterday, today and tomorrow. He never changes. We waiver back and forth, fade in and out, but God never changes. His trust is unconditional and always available. In trusting him, there is safety, blessings, guidance and mercy.

My Buckler. In the natural, a buckler is a shield but when translated into God's domain it signifies God's truth and help. It works as a shield to protect and guide. Easy to imagine or picture a shield covering the body to repel stones, darts or physical assaults. However, with God as buckler the entire body, mind and spirit is covered, draped in His truth and help to repel any assaults from the enemy so any strategies from the principalities of darkness will bounce off— will eliminate them from being taken into our spirit and cause damage. God is always fighting for us, defending us at great odds so we can overcome and have victories. If God be for us, who can be against us? Whom shall we fear? The promises of the Psalms always remain steadfast.

The Horn. Think of power and strength from the blast of a horn. It gets attention. It summons. It announces something is going on. God wants our attention. He summons us to heed His calling. He announces things are happening as He did in days of old with the prophets to alert people to be aware, be ready, be prepared—and do not fear. It is through His power and strength we are girded up for battle—to fight the foe—remain resilient and win the victory. Joel 2:1, is well known for its 'blowing the trumpet and sounding an alarm in His holy mountain..' Also Habakkuk 3:4, exemplifying God's strength by 'horns coming out of His hand.'

My Salvation. The Gift that is a Gift all to itself. The Gift given to mankind by Jesus in the sacrificial act accomplished on the cross. A promise given since the time of Adam. Revealed by the prophets.

Promised to the Gentiles. Salvation available to all found in God's grace, love and mercy. Salvation—to be restored, set free from sin, to live with eternal promise of being forever in heaven with Father, Son and Holy Spirit.

My High Tower. What an imposing thought! What an image of protection, being safeguarded and being watched over and from above by a mighty and sovereign God. A mighty God who is omniscient and omnipresent, faithful, everlasting, holy and true. He goes to the heights to care for His children. He is extreme in His pursuit to be above everything exhibiting strength and being formidable as a tower projects itself. Yes, there are more than just these ten gifts given by Abba, Father, but to these amassed in one verse is quite significant in him telling us and showing us His great love. To God be all honor, glory and praise—and thanksgiving. Amen.

7

DRINKING FROM MY SAUCER

BECAUSE MY CUP IS OVERFLOWED

"I think I will drink my tea with a saucer in the future to remind myself of the Lord's goodness."
—JEANINE RANDALL

Stunning words from a song I just heard, *Drinking From My Saucer* [1]by Michael Combs. Oh! To be so appreciative of God's mercies overflowing to consume even the extras that spill over the rim of a cup into a saucer.

Oh! To have that thirst and desire to not let a single drop go to waste. Oh! To disregard etiquette and lavish oneself in the abundance of God. Oh! To be child-like and sincere like my granddaughter lapping her plate because the food was so good.

Calvary shouts of God's mercies when Jesus lavishly spilled His blood —every drop from Gethsemane to the Cross—and provided saucers for all His children to not just be blessed, but blessed to overflowing.

To be so blessed, saucers are provided in our lives to catch the overflow. Saucers are needed to satiate our thirst even to the extreme of lapping our plates.

Remember, Jesus was not considering etiquette or social manners when He told His Father He would accept the cup offered him. He had no regard for society and its phony veneers; protocols set by the 'establishment' so He would be politically correct. His regard was to present salvation to mankind that had fallen corrupt to the attachments and deceptive ways of the world. He was thinking saucers.

He knew the miracle and eternal effects of Calvary would create an impact in people's minds and hearts, which would lead them to lapping their plates. They just had to choose.

Mankind needed to engage the righteous motor intended to direct free will and make choices of permanency and eternity, not temporary and fleeting decisions resulting in futility. Mankind needed a sacrifice unmatched by any other and so perfect it would never be repeated again.

He created life. He gave His life.

What of the saucers in our lives?

Do we have them properly placed under our cups to catch any and all overflowing mercies from God? Do we limit God by just setting out a cup—even a large one—and thinking it sufficient to change our flesh and Adamic nature? Can we not grasp the concept His mercies are new every morning and so abundant—regardless of status—that saucers are necessary to catch the drippings?

Jesus' parables are rampant with story lines of giving all, unconditionally. Such stories that run applicable analogies to our lives today. Lessons to teach, edify and encourage. He was pure, holy and truthful.

Would He be less significant in His Calvary experience?

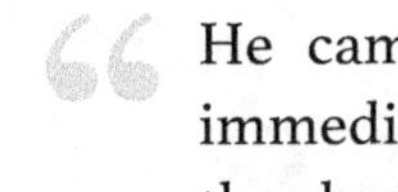 He came to teach, save and set people free in His immediate environment—in His 'earthly' life, trodding the dusty roads with well-worn sandals, robe flapping, taking time to drink and sup with harlots, tax collectors, high society and low society.

He was not a respecter of persons. He did not delegate saucers to a select or elite few. He said, "Come". Learn of Me and what is not learned I will exemplify by love on the Cross.

Saucers—round, oval, square, deep with edges for picking up and lapping to quench our spiritual palates.

Saucers.

Will you pick up your saucer today?

Will you drink and lap every drop, then praise and thank God for His enduring faithfulness?

Will you disregard the world's etiquette and political correctness and be like the deer panting for the water stream?

Jesus is waiting for us.

Waiting to partake, as my granddaughter, so none will be wasted.

8

YELLOW SOCKS

ROOM 422

*"As we go through this life there are many people that we meet.
Very few have an impact in ways that touch our lives forever from
knowing them."*
—DAVID L. RANDALL

They are the one bright item in the hospital room where my husband has been for four days. Actually, the blankets are nice—stark white with dark blue stripes at each end. It felt like putting on a prayer shawl when I covered him last night.

Like new hospitals today, the rooms are beautiful—ceiling to floor—leather furniture, computer screen and keyboard, and TV—certainly an extreme contrast to hospitals seen in the Philippines. Over there, at least eight people could fit into this one spacious area.

But we live in a good part of modern America where inventions and interventions embrace machines with pumps and tubes to do amazing things inside the body as well as outside. No way Pepto-Bismol could have released the internal blockade of toxins producing much pain and distress. The color of pain is so individually expressed.

Suddenly, Room 422 takes on the atmosphere of a science experiment —colored wires and patches for heart monitoring; clear plastic tubes to collect excretions (talk about color—oyvey!) into a reservoir.

In all of this drama, God's creation is in play and colors of release and relief emerge.

The body is designed with openings and passages to interplay and allow tubing inserted in a nostril to find its way through the hallways of organs and reach the end of the body. A suction pump produces immediate results as murky liquid—dark green, brown—starts racing from inside the body surging through the coiled tube into a container.

So much of this scenario speaking of God's ways in Isaiah of being higher and better than our ways, except when they look like this and it makes our hurting hearts question.

Mister Rogers might have liked this display of science to explain the wonders of God and man's intellect collaborating in such harmony. However, the harmony of a hospital room drama is a bit different from the gentleness of Mister Rogers or a beautiful song.

From the events of the last days—whether at six-thirty a.m. or nine-thirty p.m., even with shift changes, colors emerge of efficiency and kindness. Hospital reputations being what they are, particularly some of my husband's previous episodes, expectations of service are not usually high.

However, God did not slack pulling from His box of forty-eight plus to provide care of quality acceptance. Efficiency and kindness have been predominant in Room 422. Mister Rogers would be happy.

Actually, with all the other amenities in this room, it would be fun and a good distraction (reminds me of the Patch Adams story) to have his little train tracking through here. Hard to believe the real and former Mister Rogers was a decorated combat veteran. Back off the rabbit trail to the nursing staff.

I am glad for hubby that two of the nurses and one of the x-ray technicians are big guys—big, strong, sturdy images—my husband can relate to.

The other nurse is a tiny gal, like a mustard seed, quick to respond and attentive. Her mustard seed appearance is definitely only external because you can sense all the growth on the inside leafing out as does the seed when it matures into a beautiful tree.

This happening reminds me of one of my Mom's nurses at the nursing home. She, plus the above mentioned, would have been nice to meet under other conditions, but I was and am blessed that these people did appear for both Mom and my husband. I could write a whole portal of Mom's nurse. She was a powerful prayer warrior who especially prayed in the Holy Spirit when Mom would have her attacks.

But, I am okay with Room 422 in respect to it being quiet and God blessing me with unexpected time to write—plus hearing from our sons, family and friends who ordinarily would be in the "tomorrow I'll" mode because of demands and schedules which is understandable.

I lived in those colors of busyness for many years. Glad I am not there any longer. In those days, I would have used an old crayon not wanting to spoil a nice, new, pointed one. I would not have had time to properly and completely use it, especially for God's purposes.

As a kid I had trouble sitting still for a long time—the squirmer. Consequently, coloring s-l-o-w-l-y and staying in the lines was difficult. Little was I aware then about a God who intended for me to be 'outside' the lines, not 'inside' the lines of someone else's drawing.

He had drawn me in His own image, like the original plan for Creation for me. To be rebellious and independent—not in a negative way to family, friends, school or work—was to leave the norm. I accepted Him, followed Him, and became independent of what others believed was good for me. Instead, I listened to His Voice.

Easy to conclude those decisions brought tumultuous responses. Talk about colors!

First, my own surprise response was to blow all natural conscience to the wind and say 'yes' to Jesus. I learned quickly it was more complex than just putting on a pair of Jesus' sandals. There would be miles of journeying involved.

Secondly was dealing with actions and reactions of people in my circle of influence. I could have put up an easel and thrown any color of paint Sherwin-Williams offered, but it would not explain thoroughly to everyone the color of the burning in my heart with a 'yes' to Jesus.

Did I do something extreme like "sell all I have and give to the poor', or be a missionary, or be a copy of Mother Teresa?

Heavens, no! God had different plans for me to learn of His long-suffering, His idea of patience and growing my own personal mustard seed. I have never been artistic or creative, although my sister taught me needlepoint. So colors from my natural point of view would be limited. I cannot look at blank paper and portray a scene.

However, I do have an imagination. Using God's technique of applying colors to people, places, and things works for me. Placing me in Room 422 for a few days met requirements of color to portray new people in new places.

I am sorry my husband got sick for this to happen, but God is healing him, which will be a color unto itself and perhaps opportunity to write another portal of God's healing power from the inside to the outside.

Room 422
Even had a view
All the while God knew
It was for this Sandpiper too.

Although not the lure
Of the ocean so pure
Room 422 endured
Making me secure.

Secure in the night
Even with my husband's plight
Because of Jesus' Light
We were in His sight.

God is always there
His cup to fully share
The Bread and Wine a pair
To show He deeply cares.

So, no need to wait
For a hospital date
Early on get things straight
Because He waits at the gate.

9

YELLOW SOCKS AGAIN!

MY TORCH

"Yet I will rejoice in the Lord, I will joy in the God of my salvation. The Lord God is my strength; He will make my feet like deer's feet, and He will make me walk on my high hills."
—HABAKKUK 3:17-19

The oddity in which God answers prayers is usually not to our liking, never in our time frames, and certainly not through some of the valleys.

We much prefer the green pastures and still waters (or for this scribe a favorite beach on Cape Cod) to the roller coaster days, weeks and months of lamenting with the Psalmist: 'How long, O Lord, how long?'

Now, at this time, seems like only a few scant months ago when 'yellow socks' were the only dominating and bringing life to a hospital room. In that arena I imagined what a profound effect Mister Rogers and his charming ideas could have created in that hospital room to make the experience more tolerable, let alone appealing. The journey of miles since then—though much desert and wilderness—created a different yearning, a need for the sensitivity and simplicity, which were Mister Rogers's trademarks. Although he will always reflect a pleasant icon from the past, a legend, he was only a temporary fix. When trudging through the valley, faith being challenged by the realities of life, a permanent, eternal resource is the only 'fix'. God. Seeking out, leaning on, listening to—and above all, obeying God, is the only remedy, the only cure to stop the roller coaster ride affecting thoughts, decisions and actions— usually none of which, in those trying times, bring glory to Go

Bright Yellow Socks—My Torch

Dorothy was looking for red shoes, but it was the image of bright, yellow socks that conjured up any prospect of hope. If they could be the only bright light pitched against a bleak and boring hospital room, surely their remembrance could spark a ray of hope to remain persistent in pursuing, *Jehovah-Shamma*, always with us.

The yellow socks image displaying brightness became a torch lighting and leading the way through the caves of the valleys. To me, that brightness translated to the light of Jesus. The deeper the cave, the longer the valley only magnified ˙His presence. Neither the darkness of depth and length could extinguish His light to keep beckoning me to continue on.

I do not really know how Job felt, how despondent David was, or how sorrowful Jeremiah became, but I did know here was a valid reason— trusting in God—for Habakkuk to write Chapter 3:17-19. I clung to that like fingers clawing onto a rocky ridge.

In times past I often queried the reading assignments about the Minor Prophets God downloaded to me. In my original naiveté, they resounded as exciting and sometimes gruesome stories lost in the pages of Biblical history. As my journeys lengthened and deepened, the events and the traumas endured by the prophets echoed back to me the voice of God. Be alert. Be prepared. Be mindful. Consider your ways. Always give thanks. And the biggy reminder, even with disobedience and being subjected to living in this mortal flesh, God loved and forgave.

One of my enduring mentors always said that God had deliberate reasons for all the people and stories in the Bible. They were not happenstance. And they were placed there for my learning. I always appreciated her counsel.

A Little Rabbit Trail

She was a feisty, staunch, Jesus talkin', Jesus walkin', "Missour-a" born Baptist. She shared great stories of overcoming the rigors of WWII—her husband in the Army in Europe, raising their daughter and her working in the ammunition factories. But the center of her life was always Jesus. She had a great sense of humor which came in handy when she found out I attended a hand-raisin', hand-clappin' Pentecostal church. Her curiosity pushed to the limit, she finally asked one day if she could go to service with me. It was wonderful, an event which created many conversations through the years of our friendship.

Not that I need any visuals to remember her because what she taught me about Jesus, about staying in the Word, was impregnated into my heart, but, when she passed, I received her Bible full of all the passion she poured into it and the underlining, with a ruler, in red pencil. She believed, if Jesus' words were in red, then there was a lot of other good advice God had scribed into it that needed her attention.

Back on Track

Fast forward to today. Yellow socks back on the scene from a little outpatient procedure. Happenstance? Oh no! My good ol' Baptist friend would say that God had this day scheduled in His blackberry a while ago.

Early appointment (6 a.m.), day of rest, thick, heavy streaming rain to compound reasons to stay inside house. Provisions in, including big pan of homemade beef broth; quiet house, no television. All good conditions to reflect back on to the first pair of yellow socks and the chapters of my journey since then until now. Emotions and memories surfacing in abundance, almost competing with the intensity the rains presented.

All of this was a good thing. A good thing to remember and be thankful for God's provisions: little oases of green pastures and still waters intermingled with the complexities of some of the trials and temptations that had beset me. Do not be misled.

As a close friend says: *life is not fair; life is life.* So, although the exit for this particular valley is much closer, issues still need to be championed; resolutions still need to be established. Thankfulness needs to dominate thoughts and intentions. Circumstances may take on new personalities and morph to different dynamics making the valley exit more approachable, but the emphasis on God's faithfulness must be in place.

David hid in caves. Esther invoked courage to speak to the king. Hosea lived out a promise that seemed impossible. Jacob did some sneaky things. Moses was left to float in the bulrushes. And the stories go on and on and well into the New Testament as God's faithfulness goes on and on. So, too, our thankfulness to God, who upholds us with His right hand, should go on and on. Perhaps the depth and length of the valleys is necessary, not to prove God's faithfulness, but to teach us faithfulness in learning the art of giving thanks to our Father.

I am aware I continually scribe of Calvary, events leading up to it and beyond; however, throughout the duration of Jesus' three year ministry—from leaving the carpenter shop to the 'finishing' on the cross and to the miraculous resurrection, He gave thanks to the Father and did His will. (John 5:30) Through all His valleys the Father remained constant –"I and the Father are one." He had a home with the Father.

Through all our valleys, Jesus remains our constant Shepherd so we do not want. We might question or fret the sufficient grace for the day, but there is always a home, a tabernacle of rest, procured for us.

 "In my Father's house are many mansions"

— John 14:2

Right now just having my own room seems great, let alone a mansion. Then again, I might want to be out with the crowd of angels and saints who preceded me, especially all my mentors, just singing and worshiping Father, Son and Holy Spirit. Maybe then, the earthly satiation of elaborate, non-stop praise always yearned for, will be fulfilled. Praise and worship not bound by time limits, multiple services and men's agendas and programs.

How sweet it will be when our Jesus we will see. No valleys or mountain peaks to challenge our endurance and obedience. Our faith will be proven and tangible and anchored in the exposure of the heavenly realm set before us.

And all of God's promises will shout Yeah and Amen.

10

IRA'S SHOES

MADE FOR WALKING

"Trust in the Lord with all your heart, and lean not on your own understanding; in all your ways acknowledge Him, and He shall direct your paths."
—PROVERBS 3:5-6

Berkeley School of Music in Boston and my birthday strike up an odd equation. But God is well known for odd math in our lives, although three plus one IS four speaking of the Trinity and our personal relationship with Jesus and His other triune constituents.

Seventy-two plus one equals my birthday and a new pair of walking sandals, desperately needed. However, I will keep the old, worn sandals, like the Velveteen Rabbit, as a significant and powerful reminder of this journey's last years. Straps wearing thin. Latches worn off. Soles with uneven tread, from miles of walking through the valleys arrived at occasional mountaintops. As the saying goes: 'If only they could talk,' this scribe would have no need to write.

"These new sandals are made for walking." This simple comment by Ira, unbeknownst to him, signified my journey with more power and intent than he realized.

Ira. Interesting fellow, street savvy, having adorned a variety of occupational hats in his forty plus years. Two impressions arise meeting him. First, he was a member of a rock band, before I knew he went to Berkeley. Second, an earthly image from some depictions of what Jesus 'could look like'. Average height, thin, long, straight, scraggly dark hair and a warm constant smile—BUT it was the hands. Slender, long fingers with careful technique of touching the feet assisting in getting sandals on and off. These hands knew what to do. They had seen service. Talented hands that could make piano and guitar bring forth life. Yet, they were infusing new life into people's feet recommending the correct insert and shoe construction.

He certainly reflected phases of Jesus' life. As Ira brought life to music, Jesus learned to bring life to wood as a Carpenter—with His hands. And it was those same hands that held children, healed lepers, washed the feet of the disciples—all His actions infusing life into people and their circumstances.

Ira's first task was an analysis of feet performance by walking over a computerized mat to project foot images of their characteristics. He explained how to walk, first one foot then the other, and not too quickly so the proper image would result.

Hmmm...I thought. Jesus takes us through the walking process explaining one step and then the next. Do not walk too quickly to not miss all Jesus has to share about himself and His saving grace. Jesus says not to hurry so the images of His characteristics would surface in the lives of people we meet. Next, Ira explained the right inserts for shoes, arch support and placing the heel properly so the toes have "wiggle room." The shoe inserts give balance so we do not sway or fall over. Jesus told His disciples and followers: "I must leave but will send you the Comforter, the Holy Spirit." The Holy Spirit is the insert for our lives to walk these life journeys until Jesus returns so we will have balance and do not 'grow weary in well-doing.'

What better arch support could be available than the Trinity—Father, Son and Holy Ghost? All working in unison to keep us lifted up in our trials and triumphs; to keep us stable; our posture upright and secure, not bending and yielding to the winds of life like the tall, wild grasses of the dunes or mountains.

Only Jesus, knowing the frailty of man, allows 'wiggle room' so we can endure each step, each mile, walking out and through the design of our lives. He knew there would be times of feeling cramped, bound up and hitting the wall; however, as I Corinthians 10:13 states: "There is no temptation taken you but such is common to man: but God is faithful, who will not allow you to be tempted more than you are able, but with the temptation make a way to escape so you can bear with it."

What kind of shoes are you wearing in your life? Do they have the right insert of the Holy Spirit to keep you stable and balanced? Do you depend on the 'arch' support of the Trinity—Father, Son and Holy Ghost—to keep you lifted up and encouraged to continue on your pathway of life.

Is there wiggle room' in your thinking, in your mind-set to let Jesus in so you are not cramped and bound up denying the privilege and necessity of learning His ways; seeking Him first to make decisions.

When you stand and take those first steps are you upright, stable and believing the promises as made to Joshua, "Be strong and of good courage; be not afraid or dismayed," Joshua 1:9.

> "Trust in the Lord with all your heart and lean not on your own understanding. In all your ways acknowledge him and he will direct your paths."
>
> — PROVERBS 3:5,6

Do you have a determined stride acknowledging God will never leave you or forsake you as Joshua? "I will not fail thee or forsake thee," Joshua 1:5. Are you ready to pursue the command, the requirement of

Micah 6:8, "...to do justly, to love mercy and to walk humbly with your God?"

Ira knows the shoe business.

 Jesus knows our soul business.

Do you need new shoes or sandals? Do you need to inspect your current sandals and notice the uneven wear, stretched out straps, worn out soles that reflect where you are in this season of your life? Are they showing wear and tear from avoiding Jesus or just not giving him first place before other priorities, distractions and the busyness of life intrude? Do you need to meet an Ira and let God relay His qualities through a tangible, earthly person?

Jesus has an Ira waiting for you. Jesus Himself is waiting for you. Jesus is coming back soon.

Regard, now, the inserts, arch supports and wiggle room in your life. God's desire is that none of His creation perishes. However, His long-suffering and endurance will come to a finality. The trumpet will blow. Jesus will return.

Have your shoes ready.

11

———

JOY IN THE RIPPLES

AT THE WATER'S EDGE

"And all drank the same spiritual drink. For they drank of that
spiritual Rock that followed them, and that Rock was Christ."
—1 CORINTHIANS 10:3-4

There He was. Standing. Waiting. I stepped onto the beach. Our eyes met. "Come." A soft breeze fanned His bearded face and teased the flap of His cinched robe. O walked diagonally to approach Him more quickly, the sand soft and damp from the evening's high tide, He stretched out His hand—the same hand He stretched out on the cross when He willingly died to take away my sins. He took my hand in His. We took our first steps in the quiet, overlapping ripples at the water's edge.

The morning dawned exposing a huge expanse of clear sky. The sun was positioning itself to provide a beautiful beach day. We walked—He in His robe. I wore my old original gray Cape Cod zippered hoodie and infamous beach hat, a hat that now reflected years at the beach showing its bleached out wrinkled shape.

"We will laugh, for you have brought me great joy, My daughter. We will laugh as we take these last victorious laps celebrating all the seasons of your journey." And so, we walked and laughed and held hands.

There is a beautiful story, *The Master's Touch* [1], about an old violin. In its youth, the violin provided much pleasure to people's senses as it entertained with harmony and music from its bow and strings.

"Who will bid me once, bid me twice," exclaimed the Auctioneer. The enemy of our soul as it held up our lives to the world. This enemy filled our lives with selfishness, pride, and arrogance until we became old and used like the old violin. This enemy auctioning off our lives as Judas betrayed Jesus with thirty pieces of silver and as the Roman guards rolled dice for Jesus' garment. This enemy imprisoned our lives chaining us to strongholds and keeping our souls in shackles until Jesus came to set us free.

Where are you? Are you choosing to remain in your prisons? Are you choosing to be ruled by the Pharaohs of your life and remain in slavery? Are you like the old violin put away on a shelf collecting layers of dust from the world? You can choose to be set free. You can choose Jesus. He has the keys in His hands to unlock your prison doors. You can walk out into freedom available only by Him.

Back to the Beach

The Rock, Cold Storage Beach, Cape Cod

We keep walking to the end of the beach. Waiting for us there is the Rock—the sentry that guards this part of the beach. It is huge, daunting! It is the Lion of Judah. It was and is a gift from God—a tangible symbol of the Rock of Ages. Its surface has been cut and carved to image the mane, eyes, nose and mouth of the Lion of Judah. Rocks do not morph in creation as other things do. Their design remains constant and not yielding to elements of life. Jesus remains constant to give us a strong foundation that does not waver.

Will you accept and receive Jesus as your Rock to give you a strong foundation? We spend time here at the end of the beach enjoying all the creation displayed.

We laugh some more.

12

THE ALTAR

THE COMMUNION TABLE

"Do this in remembrance of Me."
—LUKE 22:19

Eloquent in simplicity. Profound in reality. Eloquently simple: Profoundly real. A loaf of bread: The broken body of Christ. A chalice of wine: The spilled blood of Jesus.

Expect the unexpected has been the alert from God over the last several weeks. The above phrase describing the altar proved no exception as it was rediscovered in an old C. S. Lewis book of which I blew off the dust and packed into my bag. Inside was a small slip of paper, in my handwriting, that had kept acquaintance with this book for many years. It is a quote (not sure of the source) given me by a friend many seasons ago. Interesting it would make it's' appearance now at this stage and phase of my journey impacting God's command of Communion: *"Do this...in Remembrance of Me."*

"Take; this is my body." And he took a cup, and when he had given thanks he gave it to them, and they all drank of it. And he said to them, "This is my blood of the covenant, which is poured out for many. Truly, I say to you, I will not drink again of the fruit of the vine until that day when I drink it new in the kingdom of God." —Mark 14:22-25

Being privileged with daily Communion, the meal that heals, remembrance has been foremost in my mind. However, I thought, was this phrase exposed to bring forth memories of Communion with family and friends; to stir up memories of my pastor sons to the various ways they have enacted (Acts 2:42).

Were the words intended to pronounce even a deeper impact on the Beauty and Power of this Gift Jesus extends to protect me from familiarity or frequency? To heighten my intensity of the cost of the Cross? To strengthen my resolve to not become complacent or casual? As usual, the personal queries resolve to arouse my thirst for seeking the Lord, as does the parched hart looking for the water brook (Psalm 42). True to His faithfulness, He fulfills the promise of supplying the Living Water I need (Revelation 21:6).

Re-read this altar description slowly (like reading Psalm 23 slowly) to ingest the depths of its' words. Psalm 27 says to inquire of the Lord, which means seek him intently, with gusto, with earnestness, a desire to really hear His voice. This inquiry is not casual like asking 'did the mail arrive'. This is an emotional position of the heart, not a physical position of the body for a ceremonial experience.

Our Father has provided a Communion table through the sacrifice of Jesus. Although the sacrifice was done only once, the Table is available continually. Anytime, anyplace—our Father is always ready to receive us.

> He always has the Table set. His invitation to sup with Him is on going and not just an occasional rsvp. His welcome sign is always out.

I was raised with numerous good social habits and customs. One predominant custom was to always bring something to an invited affair. It need not be elaborate, but something that said 'thank you,' I appreciate you thinking of me. I knew family and friends would be there. Food would be good and plentiful and fellowship would be sweet. These were wonderful childhood memories, which transcended into my relationship with the Father. I had no indication then those learned habits would become so real and tangible as an adult once I accepted Jesus and the invitation from Him and the Father to sup with them.

What can I bring to your banqueting table?

Your provision includes gourmet food extraordinaire and all I have, in comparison, is a bologna sandwich. He is totally *Jehovah-Jireh*, [1] our Provider, and His only request is our presence.

The only 'gift' He requires is our hungry heart.

Bring an appetite to feast on the goodness of Abba, Father. Bring an appetite that can only be quenched by Jesus' Calvary experience. Bring an appetite, which the Holy Spirit can satiate beyond our expectation.

> *"One thing I have asked from the Lord, that I shall seek: that I may dwell in the house of the Lord all the days of my life, to behold the beauty of the Lord and to meditate in His temple."*

— Psalm 27:4

Seek the Lord. He knows the hunger pains of our hearts. He hears the growls of our inner core realizing the voids that need filling.

He knows we have tried everything else: drive-thru's, exotic restaurants, gourmet cooking classes and, worst of all, our own cooking attempts to create an entrée, main course and dessert to satisfy the taste buds of our souls. As valiant and sincere our intentions manifest, we are still left hungry.

The pangs and growls appear predictably as the ocean's waves—sometimes little ripples which can be tucked away to other days or loud, crashing waves not to be ignored. A common phrase is: 'God is a gentleman.' Plus, He has great plans for us (Jeremiah 29:11). So, He often entices us with ripples like asking a toddler to come to you. Because He is a patient God, this ripple pattern can endure lengths of time and seasons. However, He is also an omniscient and determined God and desires that none of His children perish (II Peter 3:9).

In come the waves—loud, crashing, strong and, if need be, knocking us down until we let the Holy Spirit get us back on our feet again. He loves His creation. He loves the children He molded in His image. As a good Father, He wants the best for us. He gave us His best, Jesus. We, in return, should be appreciative children and obediently come when He calls us to His banqueting table. Have your bologna sandwich ready—daily and willingly. Come to the Table, in simplicity, and feast on the reality of the Trinity to make a profound difference in your life.

Descriptions like, 'Simplicity and Profound', stir up memories of our sons who have pastored in a variety of locations presenting Communion in simple formats but with profound results. The images are still so clear in my mind, one being a picture, the other an actual experience. While serving in Iraq, our Army chaplain son sent a picture of Easter service setting so 'simple', it was overwhelming. With

Humvees in the background, a circle of soldiers stood around the Table so basic—a flat board propped up with 2x4s, a loaf of bread from the kitchen, and a mug of wine.

Communion. Easter. Iraq.

Eloquent to present the omnipresence of God in a setting so traumatic and dramatic when Jesus shows up to fill hungry hearts. Profound in bringing hearts that could have possibly justified avoiding or ignoring the banqueting Table God provided. But the faithful—and needy—came.

Our pastor son in rural New England serves with simplicity with a lasting aroma from home baked bread accompanied by a chalice of wine. He makes the loaf of bread especially for Communion bringing it whole, to the Table, for the congregation to break together (Acts 2:42).

Communion. Sundays. New England.

Eloquent is the process of home-made bread made by loving hands. Profound is the special fragrance at this Table, a reminder of how Jesus fills our senses. Each participant tears off a piece of bread and dunks it into the wine. "Do this...in Remembrance of Me." Luke 22:19. Not being distracted by weekend events, the faithful and needy came. The Bible says God is not a respecter of persons as these two illustrations portray. On the battlefield or in the safety of a rural church, Jesus shows up—in His simplicity, to leave a profound effect on all who partake. He invites us to come and sup with Him whether in a makeshift plot of land, in a thimble size church, in a grand cathedral, or even by yourself, at your personal place of worship. No appointment needed. No formalities necessary.

No theological degrees required. Just come with a yearning heart to get as filled as possible while walking this earthly journey. No need to bake the bread. No need for a chalice. A matzo cracker or piece of bread set aside for God, set apart from the usual eating, will do. Grape juice or wine in a cup or glass will do.

Simple symbols. Profound results.

Hearts changed. Body, mind and spirit renewed because of the sacrifice on Calvary. How can we resist this miraculous invitation in the, "meal that heals?" By Jesus' stripes, we are healed. By His blood, we are redeemed and set free.

As Haggai encourages us: consider your ways. Consider returning thanks to our Father for He has done great things. Are we daring enough, considering the demands of our culture and lifestyle, to regard the eloquence of the Cross and come to the Table in simplicity? Are we daring enough to accept the Cross' reality and accept the profound effect it produces in our lives? Are we daring—and, admittedly needy enough—to do as the song says: 'lay our trophies down'—trophies of ego, pride, success, fame or fortune, acquisitions and possessions—and take a seat at the Table reserved for our coming? This is unlike the Christmas story with no room in the inn. This is unlike an entertainment or sport event requiring a specified ticket for admittance. This Table supplies open and available seating for all who desire to attend.

A personal word of caution. Bring a seatbelt because the trajectory could catapult you to a place and height of seeing and knowing Jesus unfathomable. This advice is not to scare you, but to prepare you for an experience that has eternal ramifications.

A glimpse of being in the presence of the Father, Son and Holy Spirit forever is the definition of eternity. Eternity: a forever and never ending time of praise and worship around the throne of God.

Before ascending into heaven, Jesus said: "In My Father's house are many mansions; if it were not so, I would have told you. I go to prepare a place for you."

— JOHN 14:2

Our finite minds probably equate this image to earthly structures accustomed to our thinking. However, my interpretation of this house with many mansions is the heavenly environment we will occupy and the place will be wherever we can shout and sing our praises to our Father. Our Father's house is the entirety of heaven with the Father, Jesus and the Holy Spirit being in the midst of everything. There will be no walls or roofs or confining structures where we can roam freely and continually singing our praises to them and giving God all glory, honor and praise. Such a deal.

No schedules, no errands, no jobs, no distractions to deter us from giving all our attention to the Trinity. All previous earthly considerations have become null and void. We will never get tired, bored or disappointed. This heavenly real estate will never lose its' value because it is all about location, location, location. With God on His throne and Jesus and the Holy Spirit on each side of him they are always center stage, always approachable to praise and worship (Revelation 4:8b, 11a; 5:12,13), keeping the promises made to us about a forever existence.

Truly, then, will we realize how profound is the eloquent plan of Calvary.

13

COLORS OF JESUS

AT THE BEACH

""God said to Moses, "I AM WHO I AM"...
'I AM has sent me to you.'"
—EXODUS 3:14

What color are you today? Majestic! Powerful! Undeniably, the Creator! Who else could provide this view? The expanse of the ocean seems excessively huge today because of no sun, no distinct and individual clouds. Could this have been a view from the ark? Could the limitlessness of the ocean represent eternity, endless, boundless, non-stoppable, and persistent?

The ocean is vast. The ocean's vastness is not describable and worthy enough of the power of your majesty—its' extension way beyond what the eyes or a telescope could see. The ridge of sand resultant of the ebbing water is a mere significance that You ARE—that You are the beginning and the end, that nothing can contain or confine You.

On this day You are allowing the waves to coast in just so much, just enough to provide a sitting place where this Sandpiper can hear and see your grandeur. Today's weather is producing an aspect of Your sovereignty and omniscience that is not seen on a sunny, cloudless, blue-sky day. Today the ocean says: "I AM!" Make no mistake about it.

There is no one here frolicking in the surf. There is no one here smelling of coconut oil challenging the sun to change the color of his or her skin. Today is Reality of Who You are in our lives. You are the "I AM" who was, and is and forever will be. Today is not a day of doubting or carelessly being absorbed by the fun of the beach.

Cold Storage Beach, Cape Cod

Today shouts your magnificence.

Today shouts your predominance to a world that is unstable and like shifting sand.

Today shouts: "Look up; your redemption draws nigh."

Today shouts that You are big, real, incomprehensible.

Today shouts to warn us to look for your Beauty even if the natural conditions do not seem ideal. But You are an unconditional God—loving us, entreating us, encompassing us with a love that parallels the ocean—immensely huge, no boundaries, fathoms so deep we could never get to the bottom of your love.

Today shouts faithfulness as the sandpipers continue their residence here in this place. They are not taunted or dismayed by the conditions. They live in the reassurance You are here—the only condition they consider or require.Regardless of how nature's elements appear or disguise themselves, the sandpipers return for their manna, for their daily bread. Can we not be so diligent and determined as they? Could we not have that kind of tunnel vision?

The Sandpiper

Do not read the Almanac. Do not check the Doppler. Just be at whatever beach God has for you—and eat—partake of His provision. Look to him as your provider. Be focused as the sandpipers. They do not gaze upwards and see the shades of gray and obscure shapes of the clouds filling the sky with the same endless affect as the sea. They do not wait for the blue of the sky or the blaze of the sun. They are unaware of the cold persistent wind that keeps us in layers of sweats and too timid to swim in the surf.

They come because they are hungry. They come to a God who shows up no matter how the weather is manifesting.

This is the same triune God who "shows up" for us every day—in good or bad weather, in joy or sorrow.

This is the same triune God from whom Jesus came to "weather" life with us. He is the only Weatherman needed.

Oh, yes! I love the beautiful blue-green water and the elegant sun-drenched perfect beach days—but a day of Reality, like today, is necessary to further emphasize me looking into the hills and knowing where my help comes from.

Reality of life when it is "I AM" always makes for a great beach day.

It is a Color of Jesus unique, a Color to be captured by the lens of our hearts and kept in view all the time.

14
——————

KNOWN BY LAYERS OF CHRIST

SEASONS OF WARMTH AND COLD

"We will rejoice and be glad in it."
—PSALM 118:24

How I began when I was born—naked and raw—*el natural*—with no cover-ups, no pretenses, not needing any palm leaves because there were no layers of the world to cover up the beauty and original design of God's creation.

I came naked and raw and I pray, with God's help and being deposited and held into the bosom of the Holy Spirit, that I will leave this world the same way.

As in the natural I am a constant motion of putting on and taking off layers of clothing because I am either too hot or too cold, let me be receptive to God's layer by layer application of His Word, His mandates and His truths for me.

In my seasons of warmth, when ignited by the fire of the Holy Spirit, let it be a flame that keeps me warm so that I need no layers of anything, but can remain naked and raw before God—with no need of having to hide something I said or did.

Let me be so on fire because of the power and entrusting of the Holy Spirit that it is visible in my circle of influence—not to show where I have arrived (because I am still not a finished vessel) but to show how God's mercy, love and grace have brought me to a place, a destination, thus far, that honors him, that displays how He loves His children so much that He goes to any lengths to keep the fire blazing and fire burning.

In my seasons of cold I have shivered from the inside out because I have shunned His teachings, His admonitions and His ways that are higher than my ways. In those cold seasons, when hiding my disobedience and carelessness, I have put on worldly articles of warmth to satisfy my deceived and depraved soul. Using those layers of application to justify my actions, state my case, to make wrong look right, only caused me to shiver and shake all the more from the cold.

How foolish to expend time and energy trying to defeat an enemy which can never be defeated until there is a repentant heart, a willing spirit to lay the flesh down at the foot of the Cross; to finally relinquish the strongholds I had allowed to consume me.

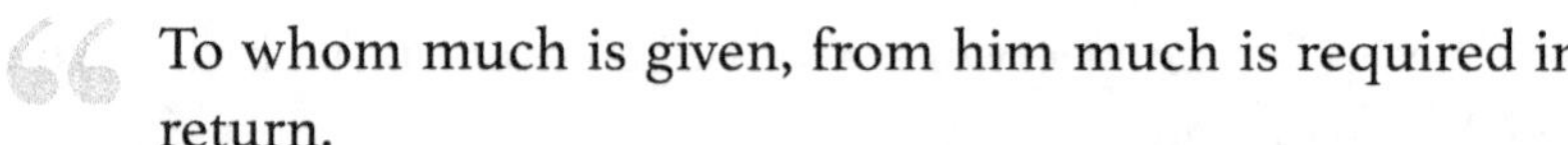 To whom much is given, from him much is required in return.

— Luke 12:48

To me (the whom) who had been given the most priceless gift of Jesus (the much) as my Savior and Redeemer, I had to learn what (the required) to give back (return).

But it is not easy to return what is required when you are buried under those layers of the world; those layers of doubt, deception and disobedience that are a mask that never truly take away the cold if you are not serving Jesus.

First, there is the Doubt of not being valuable or talented enough to do anything of worth for anyone, let alone to gain kingdom merit.

Second, is the Deception of listening to the lies of the devil who keeps throwing your past into your face reminding you of all the mistakes you have made and all the future mistakes you will also make.

Third is the Disobedience to not go to the Cross, to not humble yourself at the feet of Jesus; to not confess your sins of pride and arrogance; to not let the power of Jesus' shed blood redeem and restore you.

There is also the Disobedience in your heart to not truly believe that God, the Creator of who you are, creating your body in His image, knitting you together in the womb (Psalm 139), made you for him to love you and you to love him in return.

He has called us out of the cold of the world into the warmth of His grace and mercy and loving-kindness. He has called us by ringing His dinner bell to come and feast at His table—raw and naked—where we do not have to cover ourselves up to hide anything because He has given us "clean hands, a pure heart and a clear mind." (Psalm 24:4)

We can come unadorned, uncluttered and free to feast of His goodness, His faithfulness and His love—all covered by the blood of the Lamb. "They overcame him by the Blood of the Lamb and the Word of their testimony." (Rev. 12:11)

Let us keep the furnaces of our hearts stoked with His Word and His Ways.

Let us not allow ourselves to shiver and be dragged down by the onslaughts of the enemy.

This is the day, which the Lord has made;

We will rejoice and be glad in it. (Psalm 118:24)

Let the redeemed of the Lord say so, whom He has redeemed from the hand of the enemy. (Psalm 107:2)

15

PRAY. PRAY. PRAY.

TRUMPET POLISHED AND TUNED

*"And He began to teach and say to them, "Is it not written, 'My
house shall be called a house of prayer for all the nations.'"*
—MARK 11:17

I keep hearing pray, pray, pray. Pray for family, friends, Israel, the election and world events. Here I am sitting in a capsule of calm, solace and peace in one of your most beautiful representatives of creation.

It is real but seems unreal and is definitely momentarily, the stronger beach breeze a precursor to the winter season ahead. As the lady this morning talked about the ice spreading from the parking lot to the dune. Of course, this scene is also unreal considering that in ninety per cent of the world there is madness, hatred and terror—anything and everything refuting a loving God—including people of good reputation being in their seemingly well-anchored bubble denying the need for God.

Pray. Pray. Pray.

Do I pray through my pen?

Do I pray in my mind while writing what You download to me?

Do I emphatically put to action James' command of effectual, continual prayer?

Pray without ceasing? Pray on my tower's watch?

Pray and stay on the wall until my assignment, the work, is done?

Pray regardless of activity in my immediate environment?

Pray when the media is corrupt and spewing out negativities and immoral thoughts? Pray when I am tired and the intensity is lessened?

Pray when I am excited and words spill out on top of each other? Pray when doubt wants to seep in and fill the crevices in my mind? Pray like a warrior never conceding to battle.

Pray like an intercessor understanding that prayer is the only ammunition, which never runs out, needs replacement or becomes outdated. Pray like my life depends on it as well as everyone else's.

Pray. Pray. Pray.

Pray in the Holy Ghost, a language known only by God, our Father; a language incomprehensible to anyone else particularly the enemy. Use my language against the dominant ploy of the enemy to detract or dilute my efforts. I must remain diligent in my focus of people, places and situations. I cannot be effective if I am easily lured away and allow any compromise to enter in.

The Dunes. The Rock. My prayer must be like the dunes circling the beach and the majestic rock guarding as a sentry. They must be formidable, unwavering and dependable—always in place, never allowing elements of any kind change their character, their resilience, and their fortitude through all kinds of weather. Prayers to circle, corral around people to offer hope against the world's adjectives of doubt and despair. Prayers to guard, being a fortress around locations which have been targeted for destruction.

The Dunes

Prayers, which remain regardless of the storms. Prayers that become a beacon illuminating the darkness offering a lighthouse's safety and reassurance that someone is watching.

Someone is corralling the prayers of the faithful. Someone is standing guard. I know that. I believe that. But I must be obedient and responsible to put to action what has been taught me.

I must exhibit back to God how I believe in His promises. I cannot grow weary or faint in well doing even if and when circumstances in the natural do not align; when circumstances cannot be easily answered as to why? How come? What if?

I have not been called to answer questions. I have not been imbued with knowledge to know the reasons why. But I have been called to be responsible for the assignment given me.

Pray. Pray. Pray.

This is an endorsement of my usual on-going lament that time is short. The hours are becoming less. The seasons are going very quickly. The trumpet is being polished and tuned.

The great white horse is being prepared and trained. Its' Rider, Jesus, is making ready His robe of victory. Behold He comes, coming from the clouds. The King of Kings, The Lord of Lords is coming.

Will I be prayed up?

Will my prayer tank be full?

Will I hear the trumpet's blast loud and clear to know I can come down from the wall; that my watch on the tower has been completed?

I can only pray I will.

16

———

THE DUNES

PRAY PRAY PRAY

Come to the dunes, to hear Jesus' tunes
Place your feet on the sand, as He holds your hand.
—Carolyn A. Randall

Approaching the beach, walking parallel with the sentry dunes, which provide a gateway to the beach. The sand is morphed by the ocean breeze becoming eye level plateaus resembling huge sand castles blown over to reshape and redesign their contour to an image different than yesterday. Perhaps a different image on the surface but kept is the integrity of their foundation, their composition steadfast.

The ever mysterious dune grass has overcome multiple seasons of icy winters and hot summers. And yet, it remains stalwart in its' defiance to the elements and in its' determination to portray the infamous landscape of the Cape.

The dunes and its' characteristics are speaking to me of being resilient as they remain resilient and pray, pray, pray.

Is this not the Lord speaking? Well known for His parables, Jesus could write another Gospel comparing and resembling His children to the dunes. Does He not say to build a strong foundation infused with integrity? Has He not taught us by tangible example in the natural to remain steadfast regardless of the harsh and crumbling environment around us?

Has His faithfulness not been seen in the basic makeup of the dunes that He remains the solid foundation in spite of the blown over shifting sand.

Consider the wind, the breeze, neither of which can be seen, predicted or bound in any fashion by man even with all His intellect. And yet, it comes, calm and soothing on gentle days; strong and gusty on stormy days. Does the wind not parallel the consistency, dependability and tenacity of the Holy Spirit Who is always wooing us to 'come to the dunes'.

See in the tangible what I am teaching you. See in the morphing, changing landscape how He is directing and reshaping our lives, day by day, circumstance by circumstance, bringing us closer and closer to the profound effect resulted in the commandment to pray, pray, pray.

Only prayer will 'morph' our lives, the world's chaos and secure the peace so vitally needed.

"Peace I leave you. Peace I give unto you." I will show you in the dunes of your lives the faithfulness and steadfastness of a loving and true God. The reliability of the presence of the dunes will demonstrate to you I will never leave you or forsake you. Bring on the winds. Bring on the seasons of life that disrupt calm and incite turmoil. But it is in this turmoil the security of Christ remains.

Jesus did not have a middle name. He was Christ, complete; however, security could well apply as a middle name.

Jesus, Secure.

Jesus, Secure, when He came as a Babe thriving in a hay filled trough.

Jesus, Secure, learning the details of a carpenter including folding His work towel to say 'it is finished'.

Jesus, Secure, on the cross, not held by nails but with sacrificial obedience to redeem us from our sins.

Jesus, Secure, ensuring us with the hope of His resurrection promises.

Jesus, Secure, with the great white horse and royal vestments in preparation for His return, His second coming.

Jesus, Secure, offering us investments of eternal quality not temporary, insatiable gain.

He is calling us. The Holy Spirit is wooing us 'come to the dunes' where I will meet you. I, the Lord, will come to meet you. You will not need trip planner, baggage claim, and confirmation number. You need only a wanting and willing heart. I will envelop you in a security unavailable elsewhere.

The dunes are not seasonal. They are dominant and available year round. So also is Jesus' climate of security dependable not altered or affected by the tides of life.

Come to the dunes where there are no "keep off" signs for erosion. He is forever and never with attrition.

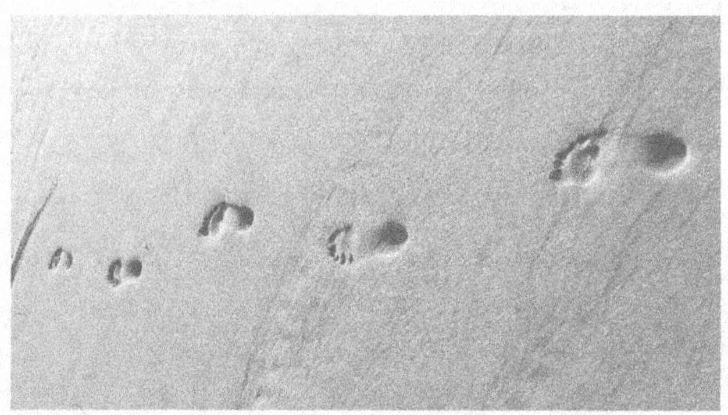

Allow your footsteps to sink in the softness of the sand representing the comfort of His Word. Allow your heart to be refreshed by the invitation of His spirit as the waving grass beckons you. Come, prayed up, yearning to seek His face. Come, prayed up, with the queries which plague your heart and mind about the whys of life. Exchange the whys for His ways. Exchange the intellectual thinking of the world for the landscape of the dunes.

Exchange temporal, tunnel vision for the permanence of eternity's promises.

Pray. Pray. Pray.

A directive that fits into all schedules, geographies and personalities. God is not a respecter of persons or place.

Because He is omniscient, His commands adapt everywhere with everyone without necessary formalities, structures or ceremonies. Many were the occasions walking in the park with a friend when sirens would be heard or a medical helicopter would zoom over our heads. In a flashing moment, we stopped the walk and talk to pray. This is not to brag.

This is to exemplify the anytime and anywhere application of prayer. Many can testify to God 'showing up' with a situation in a grocery store, an airport, a parking lot, etc. Being prepared and ready is a mandate to be followed.

As Frank Sinatra sings the song, <u>Night And Day</u>, the idea is the same, *"...in the roaring traffic boom or the silence of my lonely room."*

True, a secular song with lyrics not pertaining to God, but the idea is the same. Be it in the hustle and bustle of daily routines or in the quiet dark hours of the night the command remains: pray, pray, pray.

With effort and practice it becomes a mindset, a way of thinking second to none. Practice leads to continual application in the wherewithal of everyday life. Situations that would seem obscure or mundane become an avenue for prayer.

A boulevard set in place for Jesus to walk on and into someone's life. Prayer provides an entry way for the usual to become unusual; for the customary to become particular; for the hopeless to become hopeful.

Where are you in the dunes of your life? Are you approaching them with confidence because of pray, pray, pray?

Or are you cautious curious about consequences due to being abstracted by life?

Moses was filled with trepidation when summoned by God to get up to the mountain and learn of the I AM. But, he went. He took off his shoes because he was standing on holy ground. And I AM was waiting for him.

I AM is waiting for all of us—on the mountain or at the dunes. Jesus, the Secure One, in place to welcome us.

Come To the Dunes

Come to the dunes
To hear Jesus' tunes
Place your feet on the sand
As He holds your hand.

The waving grass a tease
As Holy Spirit puts you at ease
To know you are secure
In Jesus, rich and pure.

Come to the dunes
To hear Jesus' tunes
Melodies smooth and sweet
As you sit at His feet.

He beckons, He calls
His fragrance enthralls
In Him we are secure
For only He will endure.

As permanent as the dunes appear, they will change over once Jesus returns at His second coming.

Time will be up. Dunes of opportunity for better choices in our lives will be no more. The sand will have shifted for the last time. The inviting waving grass will be still.

Our earthly work will be done. Eternity will open its' gates.

Will you be prayed up?

17

THIS DO IN REMEMBRANCE OF ME

"With desire I have desired to eat this Passover with you."
—LUKE 22:15

"Given" for you. Not loaned out, not borrowed, not only on a certain calendar day, but "given" to us as a permanent seal of our relationship with Jesus by whom we proceed to the Father. "For you. " You and I who could be living in the potholes of life, we are "given" the Bread of Life.

One of my favorite, treasured verses is Luke 22:15. Jesus says, *"With desire* (meaning I want very much) *I have desired to eat this Passover with you."* The Father? The Son? Jesus? The Creators of who we are, and how and why we exist "desire" very much want us to commune with them? They could have their own banqueting table with saints who have gone before us, and angels all around them. Yet, they invite us to come and sup with them. Incredible!

Jesus Christ Became Our Passover Lamb

Given is defined as: to bestow, bring forth, commit. Each of the words filled with emotion, love and great intent to have us, you and me, at their banqueting table.

Gifts Jesus BESTOWED on us.

Gifts were BROUGHT FORTH because of His sacrifice. Gifts were COMMITTED to us by the commitment He made to take on our sins so we would be healed, redeemed and set free.

There is a wonderful old Gospel song, "Let us break bread together."[1] A talented person from God's creation has put music to sharing the table with Christ and His Father. Extraordinary, a wonderful testimony, but Christ is not looking for special talent or limiting the table to only crafted artisans. He is only seeking our hearts, our attention and our willingness to stop in the tracks of this fast-paced world and spend time with him. He is the great Teacher. He is *Jehovah-Jireh*[2], our Provider. He wants to teach us that all else is superfluous, all else is temporal, all else is fleeting, all else is non-negotiable in its importance. Do This in Remembrance of Me.

He provides everything needed. The Bread of Life. The Wine of Life. The Bread that heals. The Wine that redeems.

The reality and results of Calvary were not just to provide entertainment and dramas at Easter. Calvary was meant for us to be a life-saving, soul-redeeming event to change our lives forever. Calvary gives us purpose and reason for living.

Worthy is the Lamb, the Christ. It gives us focus to walk the path God prepared for us before we were even born (Psalm 139). We were pre-ordained, pre-determined, pre-designated. Difficult to absorb the idea that before conception He knew us. He knew what our journeys would involve.

He knew we would need to commune with Him to "Do This. " Break Bread, drink Wine. In Remembrance—remembering the sacrifice of Calvary. Remember His willingness to bestow, bring forth and commit an extravagant Gift of life to all of us.

"Taste and see that the Lord is good." Taste. Stir up the taste buds, ignite the palates and bring your appetites to feast on the power and beauty of Communion. Be prepared to linger. Do not be in a hurry. Savor the moment being in the presence of Abba Father and Son Christ. Let the Holy Spirit woo you to this occasion to be fulfilled; to be blessed; to be given new hope and encouragement.

Come to experience the enrichment of this 'taste' of Bread of Life and Wine of the Vine. Come with the amazing thought we are desired. Jesus wants our company, our fellowship, and our attention so He can present to us this extraordinary Gift. The only thing better will be heaven when we are face-to-face with our Creator. However, until then, He wants us nurtured by this Table. So, kick off your sandals and take your place at His table to enjoy the delicacy of the meal provided. Bring family. Bring friends. Remind them of this life-giving occasion. Ignite a curiosity and desire in them to partake of this privilege where the cares and concerns of life are put into perspective and not be so daunting.

This Table is a place of safety, comfort and consolation regardless of the overwhelming odds life presents. The scripture in Psalm 23:5 states, *"Thou prepares a table before me in the presence of mine enemies."* God, Abba Father, provides Christ the only One who can heal, restore, renew and make sense of our surroundings. *"In the presence,"* in the middle of our messes and trials—to any and all enemies who disrupt our lives—Jesus is there at the table. He is the Table. He confronts and defeats our enemies of circumstances and pride and arrogance. We surrender to him self-reliance, independence and control realizing only He has the power to heal mind, soul and spirit. Only He has the answers to life's dilemmas.

Think like the donkey at Passover when Jesus rode into Jerusalem. He knew there was someone special, unique, one-of-a-kind person riding on him and he behaved well. We can behave well also, unexpectedly calm, not yielding to the usual braying and stubbornness that is expected when life vomits its trials and turmoil's in our faces.

"DO THIS IN REMEMBRANCE OF ME"

Do not wait until the last trumpet sounds. The door on the ark will be pulled up and closed tight by then. All the opportunities to be "at table," like the thief on the cross, will be no more. Christ is coming back for His bride, to those who chose to "DO THIS"—take His Bread and Wine to "REMEMBER ME".

Hear His call, *Come, break Bread with Me. Come and drink of the Cup with Me.*

18

AS DISCIPLES AND US

SEEING JESUS INSTEAD OF "KNOWING NOT HIM"

"And He walks with me and He talks with me and He tells me I am His own. And the joy we share as we tarry there, none other has ever known."
—Merle Haggard

OH! Imagine the experience to have been one of the disciples. As the song says: 'He walks with me and He talks with me..."[1] He walked with them. He talked with them. He broke bread with them. He taught them how to pray. He taught them how to fish. He taught them how to heal. Taught them how to love. BUT what did they SEE?

Although the tangibility of those relationships is enviable and desirable, are we not as privileged today? Is not the call just as important and pertinent today as it was 2,000 years ago? Are we not approached to leave our friends, our families, leave our customary way of living to be with Jesus? Should we not draw the same parallel with them as our lives today? Jesus has never stopped approaching us, calling us, luring us to live in and by His kingdom domain.

But, you ask, was it not easier in those days? Was it not easier to see and be impressed with the Man from Galilee then today? He so looked the part, looked more natural like them with long hair, wearing robe and sandals and He walked everywhere, as did they.

He did not come polished and refined with a list of degrees under His arm to impact His successes, or with glib speech or smooth talking. He just came. As His coming was simple, so was His invitation: COME.

"And Jesus said unto them, Come ye after me, and I will make you to become fishers of men. And straightway they forsook their nets, and followed him."—Mark 1:17

"Jesus went up on a mountainside and called to him those he wanted, and they came to him. He appointed twelve that they might be with him and that he might send them out to preach and to have authority to drive out demons."—Mark 3:13-15

And so, they walked with Him daily, learning, growing, and changing. Yet, did they always SEE that He was the Son of the Father? Always understand His parables? Always accept the miracles He performed and the way He went about approaching people?

Even with the warnings and illustrations He showed them about His life and His reasons for being on earth. Yet, did they really SEE Him? Did they fully comprehend His role, their roles with Him?

Since ancient times no one has heard, no ear has perceived, no eye has seen any God besides you, who acts on behalf of those who wait for him.

You come to the help of those who gladly do right, who remember your ways. But when we continued to sin against them, you were angry. How then can we be saved?

All of us have become like one who is unclean, and all our righteous acts are

*like filthy rags; we all shrivel up like a leaf, and like the wind our sins sweep
us away.*

*No one calls on your name or strives to lay hold of you; for you have hidden
your face from us and have given us over to our sins.*[2]—Isaiah 64:4-7

During the Calvary journey did they, were they able, to see the love
and all the other emotions in His face, in His eyes, in His speech?

NO! Because, like us, they're finite thinking was limited when
accounting the ways of God.

Sad, you say, after all the involvement with Him for three years, but
when you are surrounded in the forest, it is difficult to see the trees.

With this entire introduction, we must ask, *"Do we SEE Jesus?"* Truly,
He has not tangibly, in the flesh, approached us, but we have all the
gifts and rewards of His resurrection and the power of the Holy Spirit
to open up and enlighten our senses, our thinking and our reasoning.
And yet, unless He comes up to us and taps us on the shoulder and
says, *"Come,"* we often do not see Him. We often miss Him in the blur
of our daily lives and our daily routines, being caught up with the
busyness and distractions of ourselves.

We want Him to be so obvious, so apparent with the long hair, robe
and sandals, to stand out in the crowd of our lives to make it effortless
for our recognition. But, as smart as we are, as educated as we are, and
as accomplished as we have become—WE MISS SEEING JESUS!

With our remote control, click of a button society and culture we do
not, will not allow ourselves, to pay attention to Who is standing on
the shore. Who is walking the Emmaus Road with us? Who is waiting
at the well to give us of the "water of life?"

The way we have offered substitutes to impinge on our relationships
—singles, marrieds, parents, substitutes, and replacements to under-
mine the integrity of business and church, we offer substitutes to

God. We fill our pockets with Bible studies, seminars, impressive libraries of theological persuasions which leave us no time, energy or interest to hear Him say, *"Come"* to drop our nets, to answer His call, and be alone with Him on the mountain.

To honor that invitation He extends, we can SEE Jesus, to look into His face and gaze into His eyes. We need to do the will of the Father and not override that will with our desires or accomplishments. Oh that we might learn and understand so we can be aware and ready when Jesus shows up anywhere or unexpectedly. We can SEE Him in the usual, mundane, or in exotic far-away places.

We can SEE Him in the storm walking towards us. We can SEE Him in the tomb and not mistake Him for the gardener. We can SEE Him when we are at the wells of our lives. We can SEE Him as we travel the dusty roads of our circumstances. Above all, we can SEE Jesus in our own mirrors and the mirrors of our lives.

At these times, we will be looking for Him. We will notice Him when He reaches out to still the winds, fill our cups, and recognize those footprints of when He carried us.

We can have a "disciple" experience every day. He is luring us. He is calling us. He wants us to SEE Him so that we will not be caught in a situation of "KNOWING NOT HIM."

19

FLASHING 'STOP' SIGN

IS NOT A SUGGESTION

"The intersections in our lives are needed so we can stop!"
—CAROLYN A. RANDALL

So states the sign at the police station. The sign is like the Ten Commandments, not a suggestion. God's other mandates, God's principles, and God's ways are higher than our ways.

Moses was not given "suggestions."
Mary's conception was not a "suggestion."
Jesus' Calvary death was not a" suggestion."
'Fear not' was not a suggestion.
'Repent' was not a suggestion.
'Follow me' was not a suggestion.

But somehow modern, intellectual man has redefined the word —*suggestion*. As God has been redefined, reconstructed to fit into our society, so have the "suggestions," which He initiated, instilled, and inserted into our lives. As His wisdom was subtly, but effectively removed from the messages in the pulpit, the educational system, and the world's political arena, there is fallout, a covering not comparable to any explosive.

He was very direct with Adam, Moses, Abraham, Daniel, John the Baptist, Paul and others, and most importantly with Jesus himself. Why should that be differently today? What makes modern, educated man think he is above the thinking of the apple on the tree? Does he think that being intelligent, and possibly a Christian, gives him license to do as he pleases?

What if Moses had walked away 'from the heat' and all the nonsense of the people and thought about himself? What if Mary said she had better things to do with her teenage friends? What if Jesus said he would rather be a carpenter and not want to carry the heavy load of the cross?

Then, where would we be today?

What if the shepherds were afraid of the bright light and missed going to the stable? What if Paul had not repented and had not preached the "Good News"? What if the disciples had not followed and set examples of loyalty for us?

Then, where would we be today?

We would probably be looking at the sign, at the police station, and thinking that gliding through life is okay. After all, we have glided through life before with no ill effects. We have made our own decisions without consulting God's Word and were successful. Those full stops must be for others less talented, less capable, and less fortunate.

Unless a vehicle stops completely, it cannot survey the area. It cannot give others a chance to proceed on their way. It cannot be sure of a safe intersection. Let us heed the stops at the intersections of our lives for whatever reason God needs us to stop. Let us rest, be still, and survey our environment before we travel on. The red of the sign should remind us of the blood Jesus shed, so that our lives are protected, and shielded from the ploys of the enemy. The white should encourage us. Because of the cross, we can be victorious, through obedience, and do the will of the Father.

The stop sign is simple. Jesus came simply.

The impact of the sign is profound. The impact of Jesus is all consuming. The sign is flashing to get our attention. Jesus is signaling us because the days are short. Some may say that today there are no burning bushes, no Red Seas parting, no stable deliveries, no young carpenters trading workshops for a cross.

Fortunately though, there are some crazy, wild fanatics in the desert trying to prepare the way for Jesus to come again, i.e., Dave Wilkerson in New York, Joel Rosenberg in Israel, and Anne Graham Lotz pleading the message of Haggai. To these and others who risk media alienation, loss of reputation, personal sabotage by family, acquaintances, and the workplace, we need to thank, heed and be motivated to do our part.

> The intersections in our lives are needed so we can stop! We need to put on the brakes at the stop sign and ask God a few questions.

Who or what is at this intersection that needs a warning? Who can warn us? What is the aroma of our lives that gets in the air and causes Him to get our attention? What direction down the road does He want to lead to? He is keeping the planet system in balance, and stars hung as they should, the waters flowing up and down streams, and ebbing to and fro. He still has time to set up stop signs, being a good Father and caring for His children.

Could we, in return, admit and acknowledge that He does know best. He knows the beginning from the end, and the in-between of our lives. Perhaps, in our strengths and fragilities, we could give Him the honor and obedience He so enjoys. We could give Him our attention by placing Him above all other wants. We could show Him our love. We could show Him that He is our utmost important One. In our heart-of-hearts we realize that it is all about Him in all we say and do.

Yes, to God be the glory, great things He has done. Perhaps those "great things," is putting up the stop signs at the intersections. The intersections in our lives are needed so we can stop! Selah! Look, listen, and pay attention to the moment, not just carpe diem, but seize all the benefits that God has for you. Unlike Santa and birthdays that come once a year, God is always presenting us gifts. His gifts may be instruction, advice, consolation, affirmation, and edification—all wrapped in His mercy and grace with a bow of kindness and love.

There is that promise coming down the dusty road. Unless we stop at the signs, we might miss Him.

20

GOING TO THE WELL

WITH ANTICIPATION

"Jesus answered and said to her, 'If you knew the gift of God, and who it is who says to you, 'Give Me a drink,' you would have asked Him, and He would have given you living water.'"
—JOHN 4:10

He said to me: *"It is done. I am the Alpha and the Omega, the Beginning and the End. To the thirsty I will give water without cost from the spring of the water of life."*[1] —Revelation 21:6

We need to go to the well that has the abundance of the Father within it at all times, not just the noon hour when we are cast down and discouraged. *"Save me, O God; for the waters are come in unto my soul. I sink in deep mire, where there is no standing: I am come into deep waters, where the floods overflow me."*[2]—Psalm 69:1-2

We need to be free of "Samaritan" thinking and accept that Jesus is always there, at the well, waiting for us. He is always available, and because He loves us so, we are always worthy to receive of and from Him.

"Sir, thou hast nothing to draw with and the well is deep."[3] Father, we come in our frailties and weaknesses feeling vulnerable with needs and fears, which is why we avoid other times than noon. We think You cannot draw on our emptiness and yet we realize that our "well is deep" with needs and fears. How can You possibly still have a plentiful water supply available when we are so lacking?

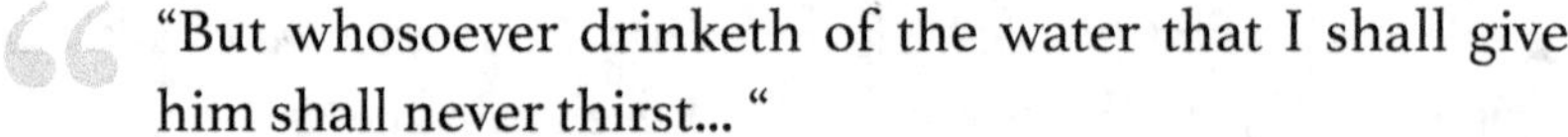

"But whosoever drinketh of the water that I shall give him shall never thirst... "

— JOHN 4:14

But, Your promise is that "there is a fountain that never shall run dry." From the water You give, we will never thirst. It will be a well "springing up in us," a source of healing for our spirits, to encourage us to continue on, for us to be an encouragement to others.

When we come anticipating, we know Jesus will be there waiting and we can entreat Him. He will talk with us even to the surprise and amazement of those around us. That encouragement should be our witness to others in our circles of life that there is water for all, there is hope for all. There is an unwavering for everyone who wants to believe. We also need to realize and appreciate that Jesus makes a choice to meet us in our Samaritan moment (John 4:7). He makes a point of making Himself available to us. In that regard, we must be willing to take the heat of the exposure of saying: *"Here I am, Lord,"* even though we might be a bit cautious by coming at noon. Trust Him that we will be in a safe place. It will be a place of cleansing, a place of restoration, and a place of renewal—a place of redemption.

> "Ye have not chosen me, but I have chosen you, and ordained you, that ye should go and bring forth fruit, and that your fruit should remain: that whatsoever ye shall ask of the Father in my name, he may give it you."
>
> — JOHN 15:16.

He has chosen us to come to our wells of need. He has chosen us to come where we live, instead of remaining in Jerusalem. **So let us pursue Him.** Let us go to the fountain that never will run dry with anticipation and eagerness of meeting the Promise.

21

HEARING GOD

NOW THAT WE HAVE SEEN HIM

*"I will bless the Lord, who hath given me counsel: my reins also
instruct me in the night seasons."*
—PSALM 16:7

Personally, I hear God at the end of my pen. His voice to me is smooth, consistent and always sure. At times, in circumstances when action and not writing is required, there is a stirring in my reins (my own thoughts) deep inside that becomes a whirl and remains. But there is always a quiet, stable voice.

"I will bless the Lord, who hath given me counsel: my reins also instruct me in the night seasons." Because of the many facets of God, I think "hearing" takes on many forms for people. Only He knows how acute our audio capacities have become to acknowledge Him when he speaks. The Bible contains rampant definitions of the various ways God speaks, all customized for the person and the event.

I have written on planes, in cars, at the beach and in my back yard. I have written in noise and quiet, feeling happy, feeling sad. I've written feeling joyfully exuberant, and feeling totally defeated. Whenever the occasion, His message is very clear—*write.*

I have spoken or acted at spontaneous times. I have spoken or acted after times of preparation as He has urged me to do so. It is not overtly dramatic and certainly not like the renditions in the Bible. In the Bible, He has been loud, dramatic, determined or declarative issuing warnings and mandates.

Regardless of the methods and techniques He uses, in Bible times or in present times, He speaks. People wonder, ask, and find it hard to believe that an omnipotent God would reach down to His children and talk to them or with them.

The people in the old days were in disbelief needing the clouds and burning bushes. Today, many find it improbable that the God of the universe would talk with us. Why would the God of the universe try to enter into our world and busyness?

At times, I wonder if we would see the cloud or recognize the burning bush. But, thanks to His patience and love, He does talk with us. He considers all our needs. He understands all our motives and announces Himself in various forms to get and keep our attention.

From the beginning, God was concerned for our welfare and, like a good parent, established boundaries. Examples are:

- In Genesis 2:17, and I Samuel 3:11-14, His words describe the cautions and warnings of His parenting.
- In Psalm 10:17, He speaks because He loves us so much.
- In John 12:30, He speaks to encourage.

We need to hear Him, realize it is He, and accept His Word.

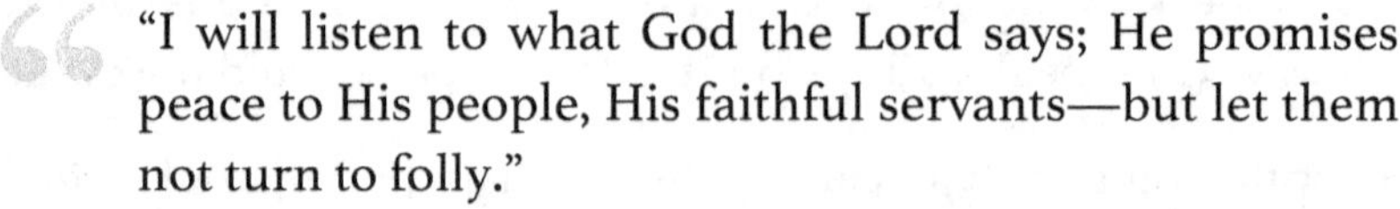

"I will listen to what God the Lord says; He promises peace to His people, His faithful servants—but let them not turn to folly."

— PSALM 85:8

I will hear what God the Lord will speak. Whether it is quiet (I Samuel 3:10); dramatic (Ezekiel 2:23,24, 25-28); loud and musical (Revelation 1:10; Exodus 19:19); powerful and unexpected (John 12:29). Of course, it would be neat to have "the midst of the fire, the cloud, thick darkness and a great voice" as in Deuteronomy 5:22. Yet, in today's atmosphere, God still appears and makes His voice heard. We, as His children, can put aside phones, computers, and turn off any media to be available to Him. May we be the audience of one for Him.

He has much to say. We have much to listen to.

He has much to share. We must be obedient to receive.

ABOUT THE AUTHOR

Carolyn A. Randall was an author, writer, devoted Christian, mother and grandmother. She lived life to the fullest and graduated to heaven on January 23, 2018 to be forever with the Lord.

"Being a New Englander, I have always loved Cape Cod and particularly one beach that is pristine, not having been commercialized. I have been privileged to travel back there several years and to be absorbed by its beauty of water and rocks, sandbars and sandpipers. My first book "Sandpiper," was an introduction to the lessons God had been teaching me. My second book, "At Water's Edge" describes my love for the beach and a portion of the incredible journey of learning Who God is in my life—a journey God had predestined for me long ago."

—CAROLYN A. RANDALL

ALSO BY CAROLYN A. RANDALL

At Water's Edge: Cape Cod Writings

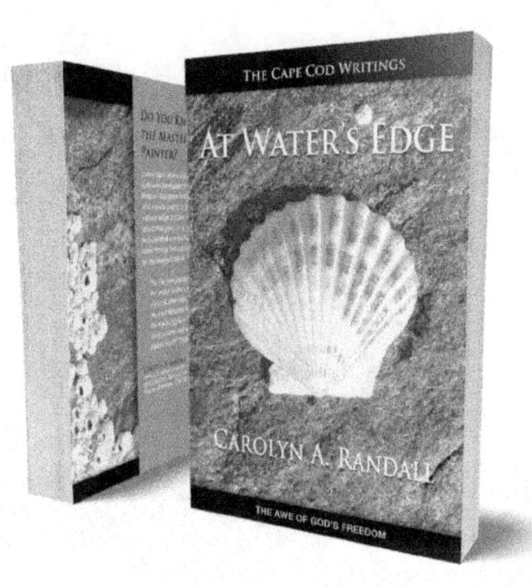

Do you know the Master painter? Come learn about a little Colorado sandpiper transplant, blessed daughter of the King, who travels yearly to the water's edge that He might reflect His glory on a well-painted canvas for the world to see through the touch of the Master's hand.

Available on Amazon

APPENDIX
HEART-TO-HEART EMAILS

From Jeanine Randall to Carolyn

Monday, May 1, 2017 2:57 PM

Mention: Aria & William

Dear Mom, it was so good to be with you. Thank you for taking the time to come up and celebrate Aria and William. Here are a few more thoughts.

Gift 4: My God. Despite us, despite "our finite nature, with our flaws," He is God. So big and yet we can know Him. From the starry hosts to the tiniest unfurling of a fern's frond, we see His glory. Romans 1:19-20, "For since the creation of the world His divine attributes-His eternal power and divine nature have been clearly seen, being understood from what has been made so that man is without excuse." As you said, "He inhabits our praises." So big, but so close. And He even cares about our needs and "yes, even our wants." Ps 37:4 "If you delight in the Lord, He will give you the desires of your heart." Delighting in the Lord can actually change our desires. The Lord will be faithful to plant His desires in us so in the fullness of time, He will fulfill them as well. We desire healing. We desire wholeness. Nothing is too difficult for _the God_, for our God. In Daniel 9:18, Daniel pleas to God to incline His ear. Imagine the God of heaven and earth leaning down to hear our cry. "Sounds like a big, colossal God." Hallelujah! Mom, thank you for these reflections today. Love, Jeanine

From Jeanine Randall to Carolyn

Thursday, September 8, 2016 8:39 AM

"Thank you for your writings. I truly appreciate your thoughts on the blessings of the Lord filling our cup and spilling out on our saucer. I think I will drink my tea with a saucer in the future to remind myself of the Lord's goodness. I have meditated on one of your previous writings on the subject of "I am blessed." I desire that to be my response when people question how I am. I continue to be greatly

encouraged that you speak with such fervor in spite of the illness of which we continue to pray for your complete healing. Your words are always meaningful, but I believe that it is your story which gives them power. I have not read your entry on portal 15. I look forward to it, though! With love, Jeanine

From Jeanine Randall to Carolyn

Monday, April 17, 2017 2:22 PM

I enjoyed reading your last entry. There is so much truth in the paragraphs. Sort of like a seven course meal. It will take me awhile to complete a response so I will do it little by little. :) There is no one like Jesus. What a blessed season to celebrate His death and resurrection. "Christ is in every detail of my life-blessings and challenges." Hallelujah! Transcendent in all ways. He is totally and fully present in the Holy Spirit. All that is life reflects Him. He is the Life. As totally divine and totally human, he experienced every challenge and every blessing. "The intense dimensions of these gifts is the verb used, 'is." In the here and now. In the moment. Exactly where we need Him. He is the Great "I am." I enjoy the visual of your rock on the beach. "A solid foundation to build your rock on...." Magnificent promise.

He is the author and the finisher of our faith. So often I feel as if I must muster up my faith, but faith starts with Jesus and ends with Jesus. "The water ebbs and flows with the underwater presence of the rock." Isn't that just like God? He affects even what we cannot see.

His presence is changing, directing everything like the rock on the shore. His presence, immovable, causes all to move around Him. God is our fortress. Strong words. What a promise, "God looms in circumstances to portray an impenetrable wall the enemy can not damage or take." He is indomitable, unmovable. Magnificent to behold.

"Our integrity is held together as adversaries oppress." Integrity-the state of being whole and undivided, resilient against any foe, any attack!

More to follow...

From Jeanine Randall to Carolyn

Wednesday, June 7, 2017 4:14 PM

How exciting! That is beautiful. Very, well done. I like the worn path with the grass growing up in places. It's not a highway that is for sure. The title is strong and the verse makes it substantive. The synopsis on the back is gripping and definitely beckoning for the reader desiring growth and transformation. Thank you for giving me a sneak peak! Love, Jeanine

From Anne Thompson to Carolyn

Wednesday, March, 2017 2:14 PM

Through years of writing, Carolyn shared writings with her husband, family and friends. My greatest joy was when Carolyn invited me to peak into her heart and read her writings.

She was an *open book read of all men* and a prolific author. She wrote like Anne Lamott [1], an American novelist and non-fiction writer. The best part? She was and is my friend.

In 2017, Carolyn and Jeanine Randall began corresponding, sharing thoughts and reflections about her writings. The love between them often brought tears of joy to my eyes as moments became memories and love deepened. This deep abiding love grew in Carolyn's heart, nurtured through Jeanine's words of kindness, grace, and love.

Carolyn asked me to publish Jeanine's comments in her book, *Immovable Rock*, and I promised her I would. She asked often, hoping her request would not be forgotten. Be blessed by these heart-to-heart thoughts emailed to Carolyn from Jeanine about "Ten Gifts From God." Have fun peaking! Love you Carolyn, my *Patmos Friend, Annie*

From Carolyn to Jeanine Randall

June 7, 2017 4:14 PM

Mention: Jeanine

Email from Carolyn (Wed, Jun 7, 2017, 4:43 PM): You will enjoy this—actually when Jeanine mentioned worn path with new grass kind of thought of me—pretty worn but maybe God has new 'grass' growing

From Jeanine: How exciting! That is beautiful. Very, well done. I like the worn path with the grass growing up in places. It's not a highway that is for sure. The title is strong and the verse makes it substantive. The synopsis on the back is gripping and definitely beckoning for the reader desiring growth and transformation.

Thank you for giving me a sneak peak! Love, Jeanine

From Carolyn to Anne Thompson

Friday, May 5, 2017, 8:02 AM

Mention: Anthony

Hi Anne, Me again. Very rainy day. Good time to use computer. Attached is self-explanatory where and when writing thoughts appeared. Thank you as always for all the encouragement you continually dump on me. I know writing is a huge part of my therapy and healing, something no medicine can provide.

I was so blessed Sunday when Anthony prayed over us and prayed about Jehovah-Jireh and Jehovah-Rophe, whom he knows where I put all my trust regardless of how crazy or bizarre it looks in the natural and seems to people. I pledge my allegiance only to the Lamb, but it is a few Friends like you who keep my desires to follow Him so intensely. Love, P.

From Carolyn to Anne Thompson

Tuesday, May 2, 2017, 6:26 PM

Mention: Aria, Kids, & Anthony

Hi Anne. Had a great weekend with family. Not a lot of talk time with Jeanine but we shared a few things. Kids awesome as usual. Aria played her ukulele and we sang together *"Somewhere Over the Rainbow."* Tired from trip but worth being there. Anthony preached and later prayed over us with oil. He has learned well. P.

From Carolyn Randall to Anne Thompson

Monday, Sep 19, 2016, 6:27 PM

Mention: Dan & Courtney

Hi Annie. Wow!! Two months since our meeting in July. No doubt, you are still on a roller coaster of activity with work and family. The enclosed was an occurrence from song I heard on radio. Working on a couple of others. Baby due Oct 19. I think reality is showing up for Dan and Courtney but they are excited. Got invitation to go to Ga. in Oct for Grandparents Day for all three kids at school. Back at Monday morning Bible study with the great ladies. Sooooooooo good.

From Carolyn Randall to Anne Thompson

January 19, 2016, 8:52 AM

Mention: Aria

Better today. Jeanine answered my note (actually got replies from all 3). Said Aria cried and cried asking if I was going to be ok. Medication knocks out white blood cells. They dropped 3 points last month so doc said to stop taking. Lowered dosage to 75 mg these last 10days but even that dropped white AND red cells. Stopped meds again. Spoke with PA. Could not believe when she said, and I quote, *"These poisons kick the cancer but cause other damage."* She is the FIRST person who finally call meds what it is. She will talk with doc and call me today. I told her there has to be a better plan because I am not doing this again. The injections have helped so I will continue them. I guess I had more pain than I realized.

From Carolyn to Anne Thompson

Tuesday, Dec 29, 2015, 1:56 PM

Missing you. Quick but wonderful visit with Anthony and family. Such awesome kids. Made decisions about new doctor and treatment. A new learning curve of trust from Jesus. Maybe we can talk in new year. P.

From Carolyn Randall to Anne Thompson

Sun, Sep 13, 2015, 9:02 AM

Hi Anne. Doing 'church' at McDonalds because of best wifi. Altho 'church' last night with worshiping the Lord in the cottage was not too bad. P.

NOTES

2. God, Can I Borrow the Car?

1. http://experimentaltheology.blogspot.com/2010/12/letters-from-cell-92-part-2-who-is.html

3. Pillow on the Floor

1. https://youtu.be/xg282my5QyU
2. https://www.biblegateway.com/passage/?search=Psalm+27%3A4&version=KJV

4. Pillow on the Floor

1. https://youtu.be/DCnUsInBQws
2. Dottie Rambo - The Oil And The Wine https://youtu.be/uyNEy8f6fp8

5. Cutting the Ribbon

1. Russ Taff - Praise the Lord (Live), https://youtu.be/6iYC55-469U

7. Drinking from My Saucer

1. https://youtu.be/WLve5I3zW7Y

11. Joy in the Ripples

1. Touch of the Master's Hand Video Preview, https://vimeo.com/130552014

12. The Altar

1. "The Lord Will Provide:" Why Is God Called Jehovah Jireh in the Bible? https://www.biblestudytools.com/bible-study/topical-studies/jehovah-jireh-the-lord-will-provide.html

17. This Do In Remembrance of Me

1. Let Us Break Bread Together, https://youtu.be/_QoolEJe6ao
2. *Jehovah-Jireh*, https://www.blueletterbible.org/study/misc/name_god.cfm

18. As Disciples and Us

1. https://youtu.be/j1ZDlBeZMvc
2. Isaiah 64: 4-7 (TPT), https://www.biblegateway.com/passage/?search=Isaiah+64%3A+4-7&version=TPT
   Isaiah 64: 4-7 (NIV), https://www.biblegateway.com/passage/?search=Isaiah+64%3A+4-7&version=NIV

20. Going to the Well

1. Revelation 21:6, https://www.biblegateway.com/passage/?search=Revelation+21%3A6&version=NKJV
2. Psalm 69:1-2, https://www.biblegateway.com/passage/?search=Psalm+69%3A1-2&version=NKJV
3. John 4:11, https://www.biblegateway.com/passage/?search=John+4%3A11&version=NKJV

Appendix

1. https://en.wikipedia.org/wiki/Anne_Lamott